Read My Lips

READ
MY LIPS

A Treasury of the Things
Politicians Wish They Hadn't Said

Matthew Parris
Phil Mason

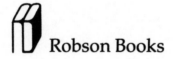
Robson Books

First published in Great Britain in 1996 by Robson Books Ltd,
Bolsover House, 5–6 Clipstone Street, London W1P 8LE

Copyright © 1996 Matthew Parris and Phil Mason
The right of Matthew Parris and Phil Mason to be identified as authors of this
work has been asserted by them in accordance with the Copyright, Designs and
Patents Act 1988

British Library Cataloguing in Publication Data
A catalogue record for this title is available from the British Library

ISBN 1 86105 043 7

Book design by HAROLD KING

Typeset by Columns Design Limited, Reading
Printed in Great Britain by Butler & Tanner Ltd., Frome and London

Contents

Contents

Acknowledgements

The sources for *Read My Lips* are too numerous to list in full. Over a hundred reference works were used, in addition to a mountain of privately collected press cuttings. Among the most useful published sources have been:

The Listener 'Out Takes' (BBC, 1982–1990); *Newsweek 'Perspectives'* (inaug. 1989 to date); *The Book of Political Quotes*, ed. Jonathon Green (London, 1982); *Forked Tongues* by Graham Jones (London, 1984); *They Got It Wrong!* ed. David Milsted (London, 1995); *The Longman Guide to Political Quotations*, ed. Caroline Rathbone and Michael Stephenson (London, 1985); *Nothing Good Will Ever Come of It* by Phil Mason (London, 1993); *Facts and Fallacies* by Chris Morgan and David Langford (London, 1981); *Observer Sayings of the Seventies*, ed. Colin Cross (London, 1979); *Presidential Anecdotes* by Paul Boller (Oxford, 1981); *Presidential Campaigns* by Paul Boller (Oxford, 1984); *Quotemanship* by Paul Boller (Dallas, 1967); *The Appeasers* by Martin Gilbert and Richard Gott (London, 1963); *Britain and Germany between the Wars* by Martin Gilbert (London, 1964).

Excerpts from Hansard are Parliamentary copyright and are reproduced by permission.

We are grateful to Julian Glover for preparatory research; to Adrian McMenamin from the Labour Party's press office; to Thomas O'Malley and Malcolm Gouderham from the Conservative Research Department; and to many others who have suggested, or helped find, quotations. We continue to collect. Readers who know or encounter quotations which might adorn a future edition are invited to let us have them.

To the late Mme de Gaulle who,
asked by the late Lady Dorothy Macmillan
what she was looking forward to most,
replied, though she did not mean to,
'a penis'.

Introduction

The British won't fight.

Leopoldo Galtieri, April 1982

We can all change our minds, even journalists. Here is the editorial in London's *Evening Standard* on 18 September 1995, about Hong Kong:

> '... It is deeply depressing that Mr Patten [the Governor] is not getting the strong public support in Britain that he deserves ... We should all applaud Chris Patten for his tough, consistent defence of democracy. And those fair-weather friends of democracy in the West – erstwhile starry-eyed triumphalists who abandon democracy when it is inconvenient – ought to be ashamed of themselves.'

And here is the *Evening Standard*'s editorial almost a year later, on 9 September 1996:

> 'The shabby mistake the Government made was to raise false expectations in the Colony which it knew it could not deliver. It was always unrealistic to expect the Chinese to agree ... Mr Chris Patten, as the last Governor of Hong Kong, said on his appointment in 1992 that he was determined to leave behind him a legacy of democracy ... It was a sham ... the actions of a man who appeared to be thinking as much about his place in the history books as of his responsibilities to the people of Hong Kong ... Hong Kongers will have few freedoms to speak of. As they step towards an uncertain future they could have done without futile gestures from British politicians.'

Could this be the same *Evening Standard*? We journalists should be the last to sneer when politicians eat their words.

Phil Mason, my co-editor, and I have agreed on almost everything in this book. Everything, that is, except our final judgement. In his epilogue, Phil takes an unforgiving view of political mis-utterance. Politicians, he feels, don't have to lie, don't have to flannel, don't have to give hostages to fortune or make silly remarks. If, then, they commit these follies, Phil urges us to be unsparing in our judgement.

But do politicians really have much choice? Don't we, the electorate, bully them into offering opinions and undertakings? And are we right to single out for contempt those who have the courage to commit themselves to the sort of unambiguous statements which – because they are unambiguous – often collide later with events?

Sneer if you like at the reminder that David Blunkett, Labour's chief education spokesman, remarked in 1994: 'I'm having no truck with middle class, left-wing parents who preach one thing and send their children to another school outside the area,' but I believe he honestly expressed his own feelings at the time. If ideological fashion has since changed, and Mr Blunkett has bowed to it, what is that but the operation of democracy? Are we complaining that Mr Blunkett has moved with the times? Or are we complaining that he was prepared to state what he believed, when he believed it? As J M Keynes remarked to a critic who accused him of contradicting himself: 'When the facts change, I change my opinion. What do you do?'

And we too easily forget that our own views also change. Unlike our MPs we are unlikely to have our previous thoughts thrown back at us in the newspapers, years later. Margaret Thatcher was pleased to acknowledge in the 70s that she was closing grammar schools at an unprecedented rate. It did not stop the nation voting her into Downing Street in 1979. Then she and many of the electorate altered our attitude to grammar schools. I sometimes think that politicians serve for us as laughing-stocks in whom we lampoon follies and volte-faces which, were we unable to pin them on our politicians, we might have to pin somewhere a little closer to home. Laugh too readily at those who express what you yourself once thought, and are you not smiling at yourself, too?

Mock with too little charity those who do say what they think, and you encourage a political culture in which wise politicians don't. Dismiss too readily the politician who is prepared to change his mind, and you condemn the very breed of whom we need more, not less, in politics. In the coming election campaign, Tony Blair's apparent hostility to Europe in 1983 ('we'll negotiate a withdrawal from the EEC, which has drained our natural resources and destroyed jobs'), and his one-time opposition to nuclear weapons, will no doubt be trotted out by his opponents and choroused with glee. But are those who join the chorus saying they would prefer that he had stuck to his early opinions? Or kept silent about them?

Since the dawn of man every politician has been torn between a wish to say something memorable, and a terror of saying something which is remembered. They do want to sound significant but they don't want to give hostages to fortune. All too often, fortune has found them out, but still I feel a sneaking preference for the man or woman with the intellectual courage to risk the mockery of future events, and to say what they think now.

Nor should we forget that what the press too easily calls a 'gaffe' may have been true at the time. In mid-press conference in the heat of the 1992 election battle, the temptation for John Major to say 'we will not widen the scope of VAT' must have been immense, but he did not say that. He said 'we have no plans to widen the scope of VAT' and it is very possible that this was true. Little good that careful phrasing did him, for the words have been repeated a thousand times against him, ever since changing circumstances provoked a change of policy.

I must confess a certain admiration, too, for some of those who coined what many readers will regard as the silliest utterances in this book. Dangerous as it is to nail your colours to an ideological mast, it is riskier still to commit yourself to opinions about the future of science or technology. Yet those who railed against the extinction of the horse in modern warfare, warned against the moral dangers of broadcasting, pronounced that nothing good would ever come of motor cars or delivered themselves of the opinion that civil aviation would never fly, are among the most lovable of this book's dramatis personae.

Phil Mason keeps what is probably the world's best collection of such gems and we reprint just a few of them here in a chapter of their own, entitled 'Uh? They Cannot Be Serious'. When in 1928 Major Hills MP told the House of Commons 'the aeroplane has only little, or very limited future', or when in 1921 Major General Seely warned the House that 'the Secretary of State's advisers are quite wrong in thinking they can substitute tanks for cavalry; every advance of science has made the horse a more and more indispensable weapon of war,' did either of them stop to think their wisdom might grace an anthology such as this?

We called our anthology Read My Lips in homage to George Bush, who coined it when promising 'no new taxes'. He imposed them later. Ranging across the globe and the centuries, our aim is to remind readers of old favourites (Alec Douglas-Home in 1962: 'I could never be Prime Minister: I do all my sums with matchsticks'); current favourites ('job insecurity is a state of mind', – Ian Lang, President of the Board of Trade) and some little-known finds like Labour's present Chief Whip, Donald Dewar, who said of what we now call the world's most successful airline: 'British Airways will be the pantomime horse of capitalism.' That was in 1979, just before privatization.

Harold Wilson's famous 'the pound in your pocket' is here, as are less familiar finds. A prediction from the ousted Cuban dictator Fulgencio Batista ('I give Castro a year, no longer') – in 1959 – is remembered now by few but Fidel Castro himself, now in his fourth decade of power. And who these days but Phil Mason can quote a certain Mr Henniker-Major MP who, speaking on slavery in 1798, told fellow MPs: 'They are conveyed from a country of barbarous superstition to a land of civilization and humanity. In my opinion, therefore, the clamours against the trade are groundless.'

Henniker Major would find no supporters now and we rejoice that his views then did not prevail. But he had a point. And examples do occur in this book where, though the world has ridiculed a politician for his supposed nonsense, his real folly has been to be too clever for his audience. In oratory, irony and paradox are dangerous weapons and too often boomerang. When Keith Joseph remarked that he wanted more inequality in society, as this would benefit the poor, the aphorism was neither thoughtless nor absurd – though, depending on your economics, you may not agree with him. Sir Keith, however, was simply laughed at.

Providing structure for what can only be a random collection has been a challenge. Alphabetical or chronological lists are without meaning and there's often benefit in placing side by side quotes from different people (or even different eras) to illustrate a train of thought – or folly. Under the broad classification of what we might call regrettable utterances can be placed a number of distinct kinds of mistake, so within our anthology we have tried to categorize. Dear reader, waste no time in observing that the borders between categories are indistinct, sometimes illogical, and often transgressed below. We know. We do not much care. The aim has been to provide some kind of shape to our anthology. But no amount of intellectual tailoring can prevent the occasional lump, tuck or fold.

A broad structure does, nevertheless, emerge. One distinction is between utterances which were always and self-evidently absurd, and those which only become so in retrospect. Remarks which raised no eyebrows at the time have often been rendered ridiculous by developments the speaker never foresaw. 'The United States will not be a threat to us for decades' (Hitler, 12 November 1940) is an example. We've called this chapter 'Er ... If Only They'd Known.

Some statements have had the rug pulled from under them, not by outside events, but by the speaker himself in a subsequent change of attitude. 'A scandalous and undemocratic measure against the trade union movement,' said Tony Blair in 1983, offering his view on the Tory industrial relations legislation. 'Heavens above, that is common sense,' he said twelve years later, of the same legislation. We've called this chapter 'Well ... On Second Thoughts'.

And then there are direct undertakings – overtaken, so to speak, by a reversal of the speaker's own intentions. 'Ahem I May Have Misled You' is the title of our chapter on broken pledges. 'I fight on. I fight to win,' declared Margaret Thatcher, shortly before retiring from the leadership contest. Under the heading of 'Moi? Ambitions Disavowed' we have chronicled the almost unvarying habit in politics of insisting that you will never be a candidate for the very office you subsequently fight tooth and nail to achieve. 'I'd rather bungee jump without the cord,' said Ross Perot. As I write, he is making plans to do so.

A variety of verbal outrage we found difficult to categorize consists of statements from politicians temporarily bereft of their political antennae, which just leave us winded by their cheek. 'Son, they're *all* my helicopters,' said President Johnson to an airman who presumed to direct him to his helicopter. We decided on the title 'Oh! Sheer Bloody Nerve. Under 'Ouch – Sitting Ducks' we've collected some of the open goals which invited others to score memorably. Dismissed as a minister by Macmillan, Viscount Kilmuir complained that even a cook would have been treated with more consideration. Macmillan murmured that competent cooks were hard to find.

Not every verbal gaffe, of course, is a mistake. That it was a mistake to *say* it does not of itself make it false. Or it may honestly represent the speaker's real – if appalling – view. Our chapter 'Shh! Giving the Game Away' collects a few prize sayings which, true or false, were better left unsaid. 'What's a skirt but an open gateway?' asked the late Sir Nicholas Fairbairn MP, a former Scottish Solicitor-General.

As for the range of verbal infelicities we found hardest to classify, our chapter heading reflects our bafflement: 'Eh Come Again?' These include what Private Eye likes to call Colemanballs. 'I have the thermometer in my mouth and I'm listening to it all the time,' was how William Whitelaw chose to reassure someone worried about Party morale.

But my favourite chapter is the least complicated: verbal balls-ups. We've called it 'Oops! Simple Blunders'. 'At Consett you have got one of the best steelworks in Europe,' Kenneth Clarke, Chancellor of the Exchequer, told the bemused residents of that town, fifteen years after the steelworks had closed. 'How nice to see you all here,' said Roy Jenkins to a group of prisoners on his visit to their jail. 'Do you like the work?' President Nixon asked a policeman lying injured in the road after an accident to his presidential motorcade. 'This is a great day for France,' said Nixon at President Pompidou's funeral. 'Once you've seen one ghetto, you've seen them all' – that was Nixon's Vice-president, Spiro Agnew. The phrase returned to haunt him.

Come to think of it, this is an anthology of verbal haunting. Ask Norman Tebbit, whose recollection in 1981 of his dear old dad – 'he didn't riot: he got on a bike and looked for work' – has never been exorcised. It was around that time that Roy Jenkins, later to start the SDP then join the Liberal Democrats said: 'The Labour Party always is and has been an instinctive part of my life.'

What foresight. A foresight shared a decade earlier by Margaret Thatcher: 'No woman, in my time, will be Prime Minister.' I'm glad she was wrong. It would be a great shame if anyone saw the making of a rash undertaking as any reason to stick to it. Should Chris Patten feel remotely miffed with me for digging up his 1988 prophecy – 'What I know is that I shall only ever be the Member of Parliament for Bath. No Plumshire North for me' – I conclude this introduction with the hope that he never feels bound by it.

But Phil is right: we are entitled to a smirk or two. He and I trust this book provokes many such.

Matthew Parris

1 *Oops!*

Simple Blunders

Need we say more ... ?

Exchange between first ladies during visit by Harold Macmillan to Paris to mark General de Gaulle's retirement:

Dorothy Macmillan: What are you looking forward to now?
Madame de Gaulle: A penis.
General de Gaulle: My dear, I think the English don't pronounce the word quite like that. It's not 'a penis', but 'appiness'.

This is a great day for France.

Richard Nixon, in Paris for the funeral of President Pompidou, 1974

To His Majesty the King of Sweden!

James Callaghan, Foreign Secretary, proposing a toast to his host at a dinner in Oslo, Norway

[You are] a worthy representative of the new democracy in Brazil.

Callaghan, Prime Minister, toasting General Ramalho Eanes, President of Portugal, summit meeting of leaders of NATO (of which Brazil is not a member), London, May 1977

It is marvellous to be in South Island.

The Duke of Devonshire, Foreign Office minister in Macmillan's government, on arrival in North Island, New Zealand

It's good to be in the capital.

Duchess of York, greeting Rudolph Giuliani, Mayor of New York

It's nice to be in Devon again.
(*Party supporter: It's Cornwall.*)

Paddy Ashdown arriving in Saltash, Cornwall, general election campaign 1992

You too have difficulties with unemployment in the United States.

Margaret Thatcher – while visiting Canada, 1982

Either you act firmly against drug traffickers, or I close the borders.

Jacques Chirac, French President, to Wim Kok, Dutch Prime Minister at a summit, 1995. (France and Holland do not share a border.)

How are you, Mr Mayor? I'm glad to meet you.

Ronald Reagan failing to recognize his own Secretary for Housing and Urban Development, Samuel Pierce, at a White House reception for US mayors, 1981

To President Figueiredo and the people of Bolivia ... I mean Brazil. Bolivia's where I'm going next.

Reagan, toasting his host in Brasilia, 1982. (He was going to Colombia. Bolivia was not on the itinerary.)

I would like to extend a warm welcome to Chairman Mo.

Reagan, toasting Liberian President, Samuel Doe, 1982

Nice to see you again, Mr Ambassador.

Reagan greeting (for the first time) Denis Healey, Labour's foreign affairs spokesman, visit to White House, 1987

What's in a name? I'm sorry.

Mary Robinson, Irish President, at a state banquet in Washington, apologizing to her host President Clinton whom she had called President Kennedy, June 1996

It was an honour to welcome the distinguished Prime Minister of India.

US senator **Jesse Helms**, chairman of the Senate foreign relations committee, briefing the press after a meeting with Benazir Bhutto, Prime Minister of Pakistan, 1995

Kim Jong the Second

Helms referring to North Korean leader Kim Jong Il, 1995

I take pride in the words, *Ich bin ein Berliner* [I am a doughnut].

President **John Kennedy**, at the Berlin Wall, June 1963. (What he meant to say – 'I am a Berliner' - should have been '*Ich bin Berliner*'. Adding the indefinite article '*ein*' turned it into a description of a traditional central European sticky bun.)

On this beautiful Irish day, I feel like a real Dub. Is that what I'm supposed to say?

President **Bill Clinton**, addressing an audience of Dubliners during his visit to Ireland, December 1995

That's fine phonetically, but you're missing just a little bit.

Vice-President **Dan Quayle**, adding an 'e' to 'potato' written by a sixth-grade pupil, Trenton, New Jersey, June 1992

This is Pearl Harbor Day. Forty-seven years ago to this very day, we were hit and hit hard at Pearl Harbor.

George Bush, campaigning for the presidency, speaking to the American Legion in Louisville, Kentucky, on 7 September 1988, three months before the actual anniversary on 7 December.

Is the West Bank a publicly or privately owned institution?

Enzo Scotti, short-serving Italian foreign minister – just 25 days – raising a query on a briefing paper on the Israeli-occupied territories, reported *The Times*, 1992

Wait a minute, I'm not interested in agriculture – I want the military stuff.

William Scott, Virginia senator in 1970s, interrupting a briefing from Pentagon officials when they began talking of (missile) silos

Do you like the work?

Richard Nixon, first words to a member of his police escort team lying injured in the road after an accident involving the Presidential motorcade, St Petersburg, Florida, 1970

I note the tremendous progress of this city. The Mayor was telling me in the last twelve years … you have had practically a doubling of population. Where has this progress come from? That progress has not come primarily from government, but it has come from the activities of hundreds of thousands of individual Mississippians …

Richard Nixon, campaigning in Mississippi, 1960

You certainly can't say that the people of Dallas haven't given you a nice welcome.

Nellie Connally, wife of John Connally, Governor of Texas, to President Kennedy on arrival in Dallas. He was assassinated hours later, November 1963

How did I know the B-1 bomber was an aeroplane? I thought it was vitamins for the troops.

Ronald Reagan

My fellow Americans, yesterday the Polish government, a military dictatorship, a bunch of no-good lousy bums …

Reagan, voice test for radio statement, inadvertently broadcast, 1981

My fellow Americans, I'm pleased to tell you today that I've signed legislation that will outlaw Russia forever. We begin bombing in five minutes.

Reagan, radio microphone sound test inadvertently broadcast, 1984

I've talked to you on a number of occasions about the economic problems our nation faces, and I am prepared to tell you it's in a hell of a mess – we're not connected to the press room yet, are we?

Reagan, voice test mistakenly broadcast to the press corps

She has indicated to [Mr Kinnock] that she would not be able to be here because she has made herself available to Mr Gorbachev.

Celebrated *double-entendre* explanation by **John Wakeham**, Leader of the House, standing in for Margaret Thatcher at Prime Minister's Question Time during the visit to Britain by the Soviet leader, April 1989. (According to one account, it led to the longest sustained laughter in the Commons in memory.)

How nice to see you all here.

Roy Jenkins, addressing prisoners on a visit to a London jail

I believe in calling a spade a spade.

Roy Hattersley, Labour shadow home affairs spokesman, following a strident speech against racism, which prompted from the audience the question: 'Is it right to openly refer to race and racism?', August 1983

At Consett you have got one of the best steelworks in Europe. It doesn't employ as many people as it used to because it is so modern.

Kenneth Clarke, Chancellor of the Exchequer, BBC Radio Newcastle, March 1995. The works had closed in 1980

I think [Consett] is also one of the major centres for disposable baby nappies as well.

Clarke two weeks later; the nappy factory had closed in 1991

These people have closed down so much of British industry that they cannot be expected to remember all of it.

Brian Wilson, Labour shadow trade and industry spokesman, 1995

Oh my darling, oh my darling, oh my darling Clementine.

Peter Brooke, Northern Ireland Secretary, singing on a Dublin television chat show shortly after an IRA bomb outrage, 1991

Thirty injured, nobody dead. At the end of this opera everybody's dead.

Sir Patrick Mayhew, Brooke's successor as Northern Ireland Secretary, responding to journalists' questions on the latest IRA bomb attack, as he was arriving to see Donizetti's *Lucia di Lammermoor*

I'm quite deliberate sometimes about getting into the tabloid press and on TV because I think that if responsible politicians don't do it, then irresponsible ones will.

Edwina Currie MP, 1983

Most of the egg production in this country sadly is now infected with salmonella.

Currie, junior health minister, on TV, 1988. The claim was described by the Egg Industry Council as 'factually incorrect and highly irresponsible'. She resigned a fortnight later

People in the north die of ignorance and crisps.

Currie, two weeks after becoming a junior health minister, September 1986

Cervical cancer is the result of being far too sexually active – nuns don't get it.

Currie

Good Christian people ... will not catch AIDS.

Currie, February 1987

Postpone that second holiday and use the money for an operation.

Currie, January 1988

Buy long johns, check your hot-water bottles, knit gloves and scarves and get your grandchildren to give you a woolly night-cap.

Currie, advice to pensioners on dealing with winter cold

If a competent and suitable woman was appointed to the British Railways Board, more attention would be paid to cleaning up the stations.

Lady Ward of North Tyneside, 1975

And in Frank Dobson's Camden, would you believe, they gave a grant to the Camden Hopscotch Asian Women's Group.

Brian Mawhinney, Conservative Party Chairman, annual conference October 1995. The organization turned out to be a community project funded by the Home Office, with the Princess Royal as its patron. 'We picked an unfortunate example,' a party official later said

Ah, I must have been reading it upside down. I thought it was 81, which did seem most unfair.

Unidentified bishop in the House of Lords, asked if he would support the 18 compromise in the coming debate on the age of homosexual consent, 1994

Let us get Greenwich back to work.

News sheet published by Labour-controlled **Greenwich borough council** urging local firms to use local suppliers of goods and services, 1981. The news sheet was printed in Bedford

Waste in any form is something that no council should accept.

Ernie Flood, Mayor of Maidstone Borough Council, as he christened the council's new bottle bank by spraying a bottle of champagne over it, 1980

After the war, France and England should join hands to make a formidable fart.

Duke of Windsor, addressing French troops during the Second World War. Speaking in French, he mistakenly used the masculine article which changed the meaning of his words

If we're going to maintain America's status as the number one maritime power … it means having modern musicians and well-trained sailors.

Michael Dukakis, Democratic candidate for US President, 1988. (He meant 'modern munitions'.)

It is a scandal that there are two and a half homeless people in America.

Dukakis, campaign 1988. (He meant two and a half million.)

I am not wanting to make too long speech tonight as I am knowing your old English saying, 'Early to bed and up with the cock.'

Hungarian diplomat, speech to an embassy reception

President Carter's visit to Poland in 1978 was blighted by the novice translator brought along by the Americans, producing one of the most bizarre collections of diplomatic bricks on record: (intended words in brackets)

When I abandoned [left] the United States ... I know your lust [I understand your hopes] for the future ... I have come to learn your opinions and I desire the Poles carnally [I understand your desires for the future].

I cannot think what to say. So I will ask my two daughters to sing to you.

General election broadcast by the **Ecology Party** in the emergingly democratic Poland, 1991

Yes, gradually.

Milton Obote, President of Uganda, replying to question whether his programme of eliminating all vestiges of British colonial rule would include switching to driving on the right, 1971

I'm out of ammunition.

Ex-Admiral **James Stockdale**, Perot's running mate, drying up during the vice-presidential debate, 1992

I didn't have my hearing aid turned on. Tell me again.

Stockdale, responding to another question during the debate, 1992

Watch the borders!

Manuscript scrawl by FBI head **J Edgar Hoover** on a memo to remind typists to leave wide margins (where he liked to scribble his comments). Misunderstanding, his deputy put bureau offices near Canada and Mexico on maximum alert for several weeks expecting an increase in illegal immigrants (attrib.)

Put a tail on me and see how bored you'll be.

Ill-fated challenge to the press by presidential hopeful **Gary Hart**, 1987.
They did, and quickly uncovered his extra-marital relationship with model
Donna Rice which abruptly scuppered his campaign

No socialist system can be established without a political police ... they
would have to fall back on some form of Gestapo.

Winston Churchill, as Prime Minister, election broadcast against the
Labour Party, 1945. The remark, widely deplored, seriously undermined his
campaign. He lost

My, you must have fun chasing the soap round the bath.

Princess Diana, shaking hands with a one-armed man, Australian visit,
1983

Come, come. They couldn't hit an elephant at this dist —

American Civil War General **John Sedgwick**, last words to his cowering
troops, Battle of Spotsylvania, 1864

Thomas – Jefferson – still – surv—

The US President's last words, 1826

2 *Eh?*

Come Again?

Politicians are at best eccentric communicators. By accident
(and sometimes by design) their verbal formulations can
lead us not so much to cheer or boo, as to scratch our
heads in bewilderment. Often we do realize what they are
trying to say. Sometimes they do. But sometimes neither
side has the least idea. Mixed emotions and mixed signals
produce mixed metaphors and crazy logic and many of
those quoted below seem to have confused themselves as
much as their audience.

Nothing happened until I pressed the minister on the floor of the
House.

David Alton MP, Liberal Chief Whip, 1986

I have not 'singled out' Lothian – I have singled out *four* local councils.

Michael Ancram, junior Scottish Office minister, on those delaying sales
of council houses, 1987

Er … perhaps 'decisive'?

Paddy Ashdown, Liberal Democrat leader, on election radio phone-in responding to questioner who asked, 'Which word best sums up your character?'

Whips do twist their arms up the back literally – and sometimes physically.

Joe Ashton MP, *Week in Westminster*, BBC Radio, 1986

Trouble with Winston: nails his trousers to the mast. Can't climb down.

Clement Attlee on Churchill, recalled by Harold Wilson, 1983

Jim Prior's his own man. We all are.

Sir Humphrey Atkins MP, on Prior's decision to resign as Northern Ireland Secretary, 1984

Bringing the leadership to its knees occasionally is a good way of keeping it on its toes.

Tony Banks MP, on the Conservative leadership struggle, 1990

I'd like the taxes to go to those parents lucky enough to have children.

Banks, 1989

Tourists go home with the photographs showing them with one foot in the northern hemisphere and one in the southern.

Geographically challenged **Rosie Barnes**, SDP MP for Greenwich, on a famous feature of her constituency, maiden speech in House of Commons, 1987

Many people feel that the Labour Party has gone out on a limb and lost its roots.

Barnes, SDP party political broadcast, BBC Radio, 1987

If you open that Pandora's box, you never know what Trojan 'orses will jump out.

Ernest Bevin, Foreign Secretary, on the setting up of the Council of Europe, 1949

We've just had the biggest saturation advertising on record to publicize the sale of water.

Tony Blair, Labour shadow spokesman, on water privatization, 1989

I wouldn't be seen dead saying it [that the Conservatives would win the next election].

David Blunkett MP, Labour shadow local government spokesman, 1987

When [the IRA] plant such bombs, it proves they can scare people, it proves they can kill people, it proves nothing.

Peter Bottomley, Northern Ireland minister, 1990

Suicide is a real threat to health in a modern society.

Virginia Bottomley, Health Secretary, *c* 1993

The Militants in Liverpool spend money like water, as if it came from outer space.

Dr Rhodes Boyson MP, 1987

Clearly, the future is still to come.

Peter Brooke MP, 1986

If it weren't for these troubles, Ireland would be a very happy place.

Lord Brookeborough, Ulster Minister of Commerce with special responsibilities for tourism, 1970

No one would go to Hitler's funeral if he was alive today.

Ron Brown MP, local news, London, 1989

She wasn't an ardent feminist. She was very beautiful.

Norman Buchan MP, on the death of socialist Jennie Lee, Labour MP from 1929 to 1970, and wife of Nye Bevan, 1988

★

If you're at a summit, you're trying to climb a mountain.

Lord Carrington, former Foreign Secretary and 'expert' commentator on the demands of international diplomacy, 1986

★

You can sum up what CND means in two words – trust the Kremlin.
Winston Churchill MP, BBC, 1983

It is surprising that the present bitter controversy has arisen between the Government and, on the one hand, the Labour Party – and to some extent the centre parties as well – and, on the other, the British Medical Opposition – British Medical Association. That is certainly my most Freudian slip of the tongue so far.
Kenneth Clarke, Health Secretary, debate on NHS White Paper, 1989

All those people who say that there will never be a single European currency are trying to forecast history.
Clarke, Chancellor of the Exchequer, *c* 1993

There remain only twenty-five hours in the day, and Neil Kinnock is already working for twenty-three and a half of them.
Robin Cook MP, Labour shadow spokesman, 1988

Nicholas Ridley is going to sell off the nation's water assets lock, stock and barrel.
Jack Cunningham MP, Labour shadow environment spokesman, 1989

There's no smoke without mud being flung around.
Edwina Currie MP, 1989

I believe that people like myself should stand shoulder to shoulder with the homosexual fraternity … but you're only likely to get that support if you don't continue to flaunt your homosexuality and thrust it down other people's throats.

Geoffrey Dickens MP, on militancy in the gay movement, 1988

We're sending 23 million leaflets to every household in Britain.

Norman Fowler, Health Secretary, on the Government's AIDS prevention publicity campaign, 1986

There's a whole range of things we're doing with condoms.

Fowler, on the AIDS prevention campaign, 1987

To go round the world in a week, which I did the other day, is very exhausting.

Lord Glenarthur, Foreign Office minister, 1988

I think most of the wrinkles have been ironed out.

Teresa Gorman MP, on developments with hormone replacement treatment for older women, 1988

We cannot just sit on our hands. We cannot stand terrified, rooted to the spot.

Bryan Gould, Labour shadow trade and industry spokesman, 1987

We're not the sort of party that does deals behind smoke-filled doors.

Gould, election 1992

It is asking too much to require the police to stand there like sitting ducks while wild men throw petrol bombs at them.

Eldon Griffiths MP, on the use of plastic bullets by police in Northern Ireland, House of Commons, May 1986

My general approach is that you mustn't generalize.

Harriet Harman MP (Lab), 1989

My mission is humanitarian. Therefore, it in no way represents the British Government.

Edward Heath MP, on his mission to Baghdad to negotiate the release of Western hostages, Gulf crisis, 1990

We were unanimous – in fact, we were all unanimous.

Eric Heffer MP, after a meeting of the Labour National Executive Committee, 1982

The essence of being a Prime Minister is to have large ears.

Michael Heseltine MP, *Today*, BBC Radio 4, 1990

I went up the greasy pole of politics step by step.

Heseltine, after his Conservative leadership challenge, 1990

The future, where most of us are destined to spend the rest of our lives …

Sir Geoffrey Howe, Foreign Secretary, *A Week in Politics*, Channel 4, 1986

That speech must have affected every thinking Conservative MP and many others as well.

David Howell MP, on Sir Geoffrey Howe's resignation speech, critical of Margaret Thatcher, which precipitated her downfall, 1990

There's a lot of overcrowded prisons in the south, and we're planning a new one.

Douglas Hurd, Home Secretary, 1988

I've found the future rather difficult to predict before it happens.

Lord (Roy) Jenkins, *Week in Westminster*, BBC Radio 4, 1989

How on earth do the birds know it is a sanctuary?

Sir Keith Joseph MP, visiting a bird sanctuary

I am concerned that the programmes are so short.

Joseph, when Education Secretary, on a visit to the BBC, which had put together for him a collection of five-minute samples of its schools broadcasts, quoted *Sunday Times*, 1986

Paddy Ashdown was dealt a difficult pack of cards – but he kept his eye on the ball all the way through.

Charles Kennedy MP, on Ashdown's first year as party leader, 1989

… the haemorrhoid that we have experienced in the last year.

Kennedy, on the membership difficulties of the new Social and Liberal Democrats, successor to the Liberal/SDP Alliance. He meant 'haemorrhage.'

There are more crimes in Britain now, due to the huge rise in the crime rate.

Neil Kinnock, Labour party leader, BBC radio, 1985

Young people by definition have their future before them.

Kinnock, campaign, 1992

Anyone in his position needs to be whiter than white.

Dame Jill Knight MP, on Nelson Mandela, Radio Ulster, 1990

This is a man who will stoop at nothing.

Ivan Lawrence MP, on Iraqi dictator Saddam Hussein, during the Gulf crisis, *Today*, Radio 4, 1990

One doesn't know how many hot potatoes will appear over the horizon.

David Madel MP, on Leyland cars, 1986

Of course we are not patronizing women. We are just going to explain to them in words of one syllable what it is all about.

Lady Olga Maitland MP, founder of *Women for Peace*

'If' is a very large preposition.

John Major, *On the Record*, BBC TV, 1990

Sustainable growth is growth that is sustainable.

Major, *c* 1990

We are not wholly an island, except geographically.

Major, on Britain's place in Europe, *c* 1992

That part of it is behind us now ... I'm drawing a line under the sand.

Major, seeking to heal party divisions after the ratification of the Maastricht treaty on the future of Europe, 1992

With the retirement of 'Dickie' Bird, something sad will have gone out of English cricket.

Major, BBC2, 1996

In the National Health Service, for years there has been a sterile political debate.

David Mellor, junior health minister, 1989

Exchange on the Iran–Iraq war:

Nick Ross, interviewer: It does boil down to a barrel of oil at the end of the day.
David Mellor, foreign office minister: Well, I think that's a crude way of putting it.

BBC Radio 4, 1987

There was universal support for it, and very little opposition.

Lord Montgomery, Conservative peer, describing reform of the drink licensing laws, 1987

At the end of the day, isn't it time we called it a day?

John Morris, Labour shadow Attorney General, on the government's decision to appeal against its defeat in the *Spycatcher* trial in the Australian courts, 1987

It is at times a minefield.

Stan Orme MP, on the delicacy of the negotiations between the NUM and the National Coal Board during the miners' strike, 1984

The United States, which has a similar type of voting system as ourselves, but very different …

Dr David Owen, SDP leader, 1986

We are not prepared to stand idly by and be murdered in our beds.

Rev Ian Paisley, Ulster Democratic Unionist Party leader, *c* 1982

I believe that all illegal organizations should be outlawed.
Paisley, *c* 1989

The cost of the Eurotunnel project has risen, but it is usual in these projects and the Anglo–French consortium is looking into ways to bridge the gap.
Cecil Parkinson, Transport Secretary, 1989

I would expect things to go on much as they are until there is some change.
Sir Anthony Parsons, former ambassador, assessing the Iran–Iraq war, 1984

I've always had a great respect and been very candid with her, and I hope the reverse is the case.
Chris Patten MP, on Margaret Thatcher, 1990

The argument about Labour destroying any prospects of recovery may be *déjà vu* here ... It's certainly not *déjà vu* in the country. It's very much *vu*. It's very much what er ... It's very much er ... shows what sort of an education I had.
Patten, then Conservative Party chairman, campaign, 1992

The absolute rejection of it automatically, a sort of Pavlova's dog reaction, was regrettable.
David Penhaligon MP, on the Anglo–Irish peace initiative, 1985

Mothers should encourage their daughters as much as their sons to take up physics and maths. And if they find them difficult, she should say, 'Well, Daddy will help you.'

Lady Platt, Chairman, Equal Opportunities Commission, *Woman's Hour*, BBC, 1983

When Mrs Thatcher said, 'We are a grandmother,' she was including Denis in her remarks.

Lord Prior, former Conservative Cabinet minister, 1989

Trees have to be cut down and replanted.

Nicholas Ridley, Environment Secretary, 1989

The future is not what it used to be.

Malcolm Rifkind, Scottish Secretary, *Talking Politics*, BBC Radio, 1988

Our nuclear power stations are as safe as they can possibly be, and are getting safer all the time.

Sir Hugh Rossi, MP, 1986

But I mustn't go on singling out names. One must not be a name-dropper, as Her Majesty remarked to me yesterday ...

Norman St John Stevas MP, speech to the Museum of the Year Award lunch, reported *Daily Telegraph*, 1979

Remember Nye Bevan: 'I will not go naked into the negotiating table.'

Baroness Seear, Liberal Democrat leader, House of Lords, mis-recalling Bevan's 1957 warning against unilateral nuclear disarmament, 'You will send a Foreign Secretary naked into the conference chamber.' *Question Time*, BBC, 1987

The police force in Britain is a reactionary force. It has to respond ...

Michael Shersby MP, 1990

Headmasters of schools tend to be men.

Clare Short MP, to the party conference, 1990

I had sixteen of them for lunch at the House of Commons.

Cyril Smith MP, discussing immigrants, *Any Questions*, BBC Radio, 1985

Clearly the Prime Minister's devious hand is afoot.

John Smith, Labour treasury and economics affairs spokesman, 1989

To listen to some people in politics, you'd think 'nice' was a four-letter word.

David Steel, SDP/Liberal Alliance leader, 1986

I think the words 'never' or 'ever' should be avoided by politicians, because you can never foresee what's going to happen.

Steel, 1987

The fact that we can be in two places at once is a good advantage.

Steel, on his and David Owen's Liberal Democrat/SDP Alliance election campaign, 1987

You can't manufacture children overnight.

Jack Straw, Labour education spokesman, *Panorama*, BBC, 1990

Will this thing jerk me off?

Margaret Thatcher, firing a field gun during her visit to the Falklands, January 1983

Every Prime Minister needs a Willie.

Thatcher, of William Whitelaw

I am always on the job.

Thatcher, interview on *Aspel and Co*, 1984

Is my right honourable friend saying that Wrens' skirts must be held up until all sailors have been satisfied?

Dame Irene Ward MP, responding to the Navy Minister's statement that new uniforms for women would be dealt with as soon as male officers had theirs, House of Commons, 1940

I have always said it is a great mistake ever to pre-judge the past.

William Whitelaw, on the Ulster political situation, first press conference on becoming Northern Ireland Secretary, 1972

They are going about the country stirring up complacency.

Whitelaw, on Labour ministers, general election campaign, October 1974

I have the thermometer in my mouth and I am listening to it all the time.

Whitelaw, telling reporters how he was monitoring party morale, election campaign, October 1974

I don't blame anyone, except perhaps, all of us.

Whitelaw, Home Secretary, 1980

We are examining alternative anomalies.

Whitelaw, Home Secretary, responding to a proposal that, in view of various anomalies with the TV licence system, he should consider alternatives, 1981

Those who say that I am not in agreement with the policy are, rightly or wrongly, quite wrong.

Whitelaw, on claims that he was not committed to the party's immigration policy

I can assure you that I definitely might take action.

Whitelaw, Home Secretary, giving evidence to a Commons select committee, 1981

I can tell you *exactly* how many trade union members voted for the SDP – about 20 per cent.

Shirley Williams, founder member of the SDP, election post-mortem, 1983

Certain elements of the British Medical Association leadership have gone over the top and taken fully entrenched positions.

Nicholas Winterton MP, on health reforms, 1989

The idea of a pilot scheme is to see whether it will fly.

Lord Young, Employment Secretary, 1985

Oh look – with hindsight, you can always look back.

Lord Young, deputy Chairman Conservative Party, and former Trade and Industry Secretary, replying to criticism of the government's handling of the 1985 Harrods/House of Fraser takeover, 1990

The increase in male unemployment for men between 1966 and 1972 can be fully explained by the almost continuous fall in male employment in this period ...

Department of Employment's *Employment Gazette*, October 1976

One important new area is proposed legislation to promote unfair discrimination against people with disabilities.

Forward Look of Government-funded Science, Engineering and Technology, Cabinet Office, 1995

We don't want to see these coal fields trampled into the ground.

Rodney Bickerstaffe, general secretary of the National Union of Public Employees (NUPE), during miners' strike 1984–5

Money is not everything, but it does make poverty tolerable.

Moss Evans, general secretary of the Transport and General Workers' Union, after his union contributed to the NUM welfare fund, miners' strike, 1984

I hope the NUPE delegate will put her voice where her mouth is.

Derek Hatton, deputy leader Liverpool council, quoted BBC news, 1985

It'll permanently damage relations for a long time.

Jimmy Knapp, railwaymen's union leader, on rail dispute, 1985

They blew the talks out of the water before they even got off the ground.

Knapp, on the British Rail Board, 1989

We haven't demanded anything. What we have demanded is that the coal board withdraw their demands.

Arthur Scargill, miners' leader, during strike 1984–5

… in Poland, or some other South American country.

Scargill, *Weekend World* (ITV) interview during miners' strike, 1984

The time for balloting is over. It is time to stand up and be counted.

Jack Taylor, president of the Yorkshire council of the National Union of Mineworkers, 1983

This is anarchy gone mad.

Unidentified union official complaining that action by another union had been taken without consultation, BBC Radio Manchester, during the Winter of Discontent, 1979

I have probably known Michael Heseltine longer than anyone else for the last 16 years.

Chairman of the Henley-on-Thames Conservative Association, during the party leadership election, 1990

I may not know about industry or about agriculture, but when it comes to water I can certainly hold my own.

Delegate, debate on water authorities, following debates on industry and agriculture, Conservative Party conference, 1980

There is no housing shortage in Lincoln today – just a rumour that is put about by people who have nowhere to live.

Cllr Mrs G Murfin, Mayor of Lincoln

I would not say most of them, but certainly the majority.

Unidentified Gwynedd county councillor, estimating the number of Welsh-speaking police officers, 1987

Islam is not a pacifist religion. Islam will hit back, and sometimes hit back first.

Kalim Saddiqui, spokesman for militant Muslim organization, on the Salman Rushdie *Satanic Verses* controversy, 1989

Conservative policies are the country's most important discovery since the advent of circumcised nans.

Conservative party slogan ('The best invention since sliced bread') translated into Punjabi for the 1983 general election. It was spotted by a last-minute proof check, and never circulated

Can it possibly be an act of aggression to anticipate something that would be lawful in twelve years' time?

Tony Benn, legally quixotic view on Nasser's seizure of the Suez canal, 1956. (The Anglo–French concession on the canal was due to revert to Egypt in 1968.)

There's so much more to nick.

Douglas Hurd, Home Secretary, giving his explanation for the rise in crime, 1987

We need more inequality in order to eliminate poverty.

Sir Keith Joseph, 1975

In 1948, a Washington radio station contacted ambassadors in the capital, asking what each would most like for Christmas. Britain's representative, Sir Oliver Franks, mistook the request.

French ambassador: Peace throughout the world.
Soviet ambassador: Freedom for all people enslaved by imperialism.
Sir Oliver: Well, it's very kind of you to ask. I'd quite like a box of crystallized fruit.

The twentieth century may not be a very good thing, but it is the only century we've got.
Norman St John Stevas MP, 1970

I am not quite certain what my right honourable friend said, but we both hold precisely the same view.
Prime Minister **Margaret Thatcher**, during Question Time, House of Commons, January 1989

Ronald Miller (speechwriter to Mrs Thatcher, giving her encouragement moments before her first speech to the Party conference as leader, 1975): 'Piece of cake, Margaret.'

Thatcher: Good heavens! Not *now*.

Keep taking the pills.
Margaret Thatcher's intended re-draft of a joke in her speech to the party conference in 1977. Prime Minister Jim Callaghan had lately been reported as seeing himself as Moses leading the country out of the wilderness. Thatcher's speechwriters had included the line, 'So my message to Moses is, Keep taking the tablets.' The speechwriting team realized that she had never understood the joke. They persuaded her to keep to the original, which proved highly successful.

We have become a grandmother.

Thatcher, announcing the birth of her grandson, 1989

We said zero, and I think any statistician will tell you that when you're dealing with very big numbers, zero must mean plus or minus a few.

William Waldegrave, Health Secretary, on hospital waiting lists, election campaign, 1992

Rates: this was once a problem for the rich. Because Socialism has improved our way of life, it is now a problem for everybody.

Labour manifesto, district council elections, Forest of Dean, 1976

The real lesson of this … is that women of all social classes are vulnerable to attack by men.

Labour Herald, after intruder Michael Fagan had managed to enter Buckingham Palace and get into the Queen's bedroom, July 1982

The Alliance will reduce employment by one million in three years.

SDP/Liberal Alliance election leaflet, Chesterfield, 1987. Thirty-eight thousand were distributed before what the party's agent described as the 'typing error' was noticed

If members cannot get into work tomorrow because of the weather, we may have to postpone the walk-out.

Civil service union official, Navy Department, Bath, during the 'Winter of Discontent', 1979

Sir Geoffrey drove to within a stone's throw of Mrs Mandela's house.

BBC Radio 4 news, on Foreign Secretary Geoffrey Howe's visit to South
Africa during the height of civil disturbances, 1986

I'm joined now by Trevor McDonald who is down at the summit.

Peter Sissons, newsreader, Channel 4 news, 1986

The Alliance always does better when people actually vote for it.

Peter Hobday, presenter, *Today*, BBC Radio (discussing tactical voting),
1986

It will be the first time the two countries [England and Argentina] have
met in a major sporting event since the Falklands War in 1982.

BBC Radio 4 news, previewing the soccer World Cup quarter-final, 1986

The Prime Minister was said to be very concerned about the large
amount of litter as she swept down the M4 recently.

You and Yours, BBC Radio 4, 1986

Mr Kinnock's talks with President Reagan could hardly be described as
a meeting of minds.

Today news report, BBC Radio, 1987

Experts will be on hand in the studio to make sense of what the Chancellor said.

David Dimbleby, previewing Budget Special, BBC TV, 1988

The Minister Lord Caithness, responsible for the policy of openness, refused to talk about it on this programme.

Face the Facts, BBC Radio 4, 1988

Paul Channon is sacked and Tony Newton gets social security.

ITV newsflash announcing Cabinet reshuffle, 1989

Sir Thomas More, as well as a politician, was also a thinker.

Margaret Howard, BBC Radio 4, 1990

'10,500 more policemen are helping the police with their enquiries.'

Misfiring Conservative election poster, 1987, intended to highlight the government's record for increasing police numbers. One party supporter commented that 'They seem to be trying to tell us there are more bent coppers than before.' The party's advertising agency said that it was 'not sure this one has worked'.

I am running for governor of the United States.

Richard Nixon, running for governor of California, 1962. (He lost.)

I know you believe you understand what you think I said, but I'm not sure you realize that what you've heard is not what I meant.

Nixon, quoted Melbourne *Age*, 1981

I'm a great fan of baseball. I watch a lot of games on the radio.

President Gerald Ford

There is no Soviet domination of Eastern Europe, and there never will be under a Ford Administration.

Gerald Ford, incumbent President, TV debate, campaign 1976

I don't believe that the Poles consider themselves dominated by the Soviet Union ... Each of those countries [of Eastern Europe] is independent, autonomous, it has its own territorial integrity and the United States does not concede that those countries are under the domination of the Soviet Union.

Ford, elaborating his previous answer, 1976

We are going to make certain to the best of our ability that any allegation of domination is not a fact.

Ford, attempting to clarify his stance, 1976

I did not express myself clearly – I admit.

Ford, explaining himself to a delegation of Eastern European ethnic organizations, 1976

I hope my relationship with them will grow after this embryonic start.

Democratic candidate, **Jimmy Carter**, after outlining his views on abortion to Roman Catholic bishops, campaign, 1976

... a great man who should have been President and would have been one of the greatest Presidents in history – Hubert Horatio Hornblower ... er Humphrey.

President Jimmy Carter, paying tribute to the recently deceased party elder statesman, Democratic convention, 1980

We should live our lives as though Christ were coming this afternoon.

Jimmy Carter, running for President, March 1976

The United States has much to offer the Third World War.

Ronald Reagan, presidential candidate, speaking on the third world, 1975. He used the phrase no fewer than nine times in the speech.

Our security and our hopes for success at the arms reduction talks hinge on the determination that we show to continue our programme to rebuild and refortify our defences.

Reagan, President, 1985

Facts are stupid things.

Reagan, outgoing President, addressing the Republican national convention, 1988. He was quoting a previous President, John Adams, 'Facts are stubborn things.' He repeated the mistake several times.

Now we are trying to get unemployment to go up, and I think we are going to succeed.

Reagan, 1982

We spend weeks and hours every day preparing the budget.

Reagan, 1987

There's something about ... having a horse between my knees that makes it easier to sort out a problem.

Reagan, autobiography, *An American Life*, 1990

You can believe me. I'm not smart enough to lie.

Reagan, on the US presidential election stump, 1980

It's no exaggeration to say the undecideds could go one way or the other.

George Bush, during presidential campaign, 1988

I believe in unions and I believe in non-unions.

Bush, campaign 1988

I don't know what he means, but I disagree with him.

Bush, responding to a journalist's question during the Gulf crisis, 1990

I have opinions of my own – strong opinions – but I don't always agree with them.

Bush

We have had triumphs, we have made mistakes, we have had sex.

Bush, on his eight years as Ronald Reagan's Vice-President, Republican national convention, 1988. He meant to say, 'we have had setbacks'.

I stand for anti-bigotry, anti-semitism and anti-racism.

Bush, campaign, 1988

We expect [the Salvadorans] to work toward the elimination of human rights.

Dan Quayle, Vice-President, 1989–93

We're going to have the best-educated American people in the world.
Quayle

One word sums up probably the responsibility of any Vice President. And that one word is, 'to be prepared'
Quayle

[Republicans] understand the importance of bondage between parent and child.
Quayle, campaign, 1988. He meant 'bonding'

The Nazi holocaust was an obscene period in our country's history ... well, not our country's history, this century's history ... we all lived in this century; I didn't live in this century ...
Quayle, campaign, 1988

There's a lot of uncharted waters in space.
Quayle, *c* 1989

The only regret I have was that I didn't study Latin harder in school so I could converse with those people.
Quayle, on visit to Latin America, 1989 (attrib.)

May our nation continue to be a beakon [*sic*] of hope to the world ...
Greeting inscribed on 30,000 **Quayle** Christmas cards sent, 1989

There is an irreversible trend to freedom and democracy in Eastern Europe. But this may change.
Quayle, speech to the Newspaper Society forum on Europe, 1990

If we do not succeed, then we run the risk of failure.
Quayle, speech to Arizona Republicans, 1990

Hawaii is a unique state. It is a small state. It is a state that is by itself. It is a ... it is different than the other forty-nine states. Well, all states are different, but it's got a particularly unique situation.

Quayle, campaigning in Hawaii, 1992

Mars is essentially in the same orbit. Mars is somewhat the same distance from the sun, which is very important. We have seen pictures where there are canals, we believe, and water. If there is water, that means there is oxygen. If oxygen, that means we can breathe.

Quayle

If you elect Bill Clinton and Al Gore you can say goodbye to water, goodbye to food and goodbye to your jobs.

Quayle, speech to Californian farmers, campaign, 1992

Let's see George Bush re-elected this November, and then we'll talk about 1994.

Quayle, asked if he intended to follow Bush as President in the next election – which was due in 1996, August 1992

It's better than some of the grades I got in school.

Quayle, responding to former Vice-President Walter Mondale's rating of his performance as 'tepid C', August 1989

What a waste it is to lose one's mind – or not to have a mind.

Quayle, 1989

As a senator you always had a lot of wiggle room. You could say something in the morning and take it back in the afternoon; that was sort of standard operating procedure. Here you don't make a statement and then decide to take it back. Words live with you.

Quayle, on the pitfalls of being Vice-President, six months into the job, July 1989

Another dark horse candidate, President James Knox.

Response by vice-presidential candidate **Al Gore** when asked to name a past US President from whom he drew personal inspiration, campaign, 1992. (There has not been a President Knox.)

Life is very important to Americans.

Senate leader **Bob Dole**, on being asked whether American lives were more important than foreign lives

Many Americans don't like the simple things. That's what they have against we conservatives.

Barry Goldwater, Republican candidate, campaigning in the presidential election, 1964

No, thank you. I'd much rather watch you in bed with my wife.

Goldwater, declining the offer from a famous American chat show host to become a regular on the programme

Wherever I have gone in this country, I have found Americans.

Alfred Landon, Republican challenger to Roosevelt, campaign, 1936

Americans have the best system in the world: they've just got to find a way to make it work.

Vice-President Nelson Rockefeller, 1975

The chief problem of the low-income farmers is poverty.

Nelson Rockefeller, Governor of New York, 1960

Get this thing straight once and for all. The policeman is not there to *create* disorder. The policeman is there to *preserve* disorder.

Richard Daley, Mayor of Chicago, attempting to refute brutality allegations against his police during the riotous 1968 Democratic convention

We shall reach greater and greater platitudes of achievement.

Daley, mayor of Chicago

When more and more people are thrown out of work, unemployment results.

Calvin Coolidge, former US President, 1930

The right to suffer is one of the joys of a free economy.

Howard Pyle, aide to President Eisenhower, Presidential campaign, 1956

The only way the Republican Party can hold the White House ... is to nominate a candidate who can win.

Alexander Haig, former US Secretary of State, campaign 1988

Drinking is a major cause of psoriasis.

Donna Shalala, US Health and Human Services Secretary, mistaking the skin disease for the liver disease cirrhosis, April 1993

A nuclear power plant is infinitely safer than eating, because 300 people choke to death on food every year.

Dixie Lee Ray, Governor of Washington state, 1977

You people are exemplifying what my brother meant when he said in his inaugural address, 'Ask what you can do for – uh – do not ask what you can do – uh – ask not what you can do for your country but – ' Well, anyhow, you remember his words.

Robert Kennedy, US Attorney-General, to the Foreign Student Service Council, 1962. He concluded his embarrassment: 'That's why my brother is President.'

The police are fully able to meet and compete with the criminals.

John Hylan, Mayor of New York, during a crime wave, 1922

We are going to have peace even if we have to fight for it.

President Dwight D Eisenhower

The most covert activity known to man is what the United States is doing in Nicaragua.

Admiral Stansfield Turner, BBC Radio news, 1986

It's the most unheard-of thing I've ever heard of.

Senator Joseph McCarthy, asked to comment on an allegation made in one of his Un-American Activities Committee hearings during the early 1950s

This is a delightful surprise to the extent that it is a surprise and it is only a surprise to the extent that we anticipated.

James Baker, US Secretary of State, on the Kohl–Gorbachev agreement on German reunification, July 1990

Your food stamps will be stopped effective March 1992 because we received notice that you passed away. May God bless you. You may reapply if there is a change in your circumstances.

Letter sent by Greenville County Department of Social Services, South Carolina, to resident two weeks after his death, March 1992

I want to thank each and every one of you for having extinguished yourselves this session.

Gib Lewis, speaker of the Texas House of Representatives

This will mean a sea change in Atlantic relationships.

Henry Kissinger, *Enquiry*, Channel 4, 1986

The United States looks upon Mexico as a good neighbour, a strong upholder of democratic traditions in this hemisphere and a country we are proud to call our own.

Edward Stettinius, US Secretary of State, arriving in Mexico City for a official visit, February 1945. Officials quickly issued a correction, changing 'own' to 'friend'.

This strategy represents our policy for all time. Until it's changed.

Marlin Fitzwater, White House press spokesman, on the Bush administration's national security policy, 1990

The only way we'll ever get a volunteer army is to draft them.

F Edward Herbert, Chairman of the House Committee on Armed Services

Capital punishment is our society's recognition of the sanctity of human life.

Orrin G Hatch, US senator for Utah, 1988

I don't want to run the risk of ruining what is a lovely recession.

George Bush, responding to a welcoming crowd, New Jersey, campaign, 1992. He meant 'reception'

Now let's all try to settle this problem like good Christians.

Warren Austin, US delegate to the United Nations, on the Arab–Israeli war, 1948

Those who survived the San Francisco earthquake said, 'Thank God, I'm still alive.' But of course, those who died, their lives will never be the same again.

Barbara Boxer, Californian member of US House of Representatives, 1989

... the need to establish a democratic, legal, circular state.

Press announcement issued by the Azerbaijan embassy in London, followed the next day by another explaining, 'The word circular should be read as secular', 1995

We must organize now.

Alexander Shubin, leader of Russian anarchists, June 1990

It is difficult to make predictions, particularly about the future.

Representative of the United Nations High Commissioner for Refugees, 1990

Sixty years of progress, without change.

Slogan used by Saudi Arabian government to promote the kingdom's sixtieth anniversary, October 1992

I cannot say, and do not know whether the coming quota will be the same, more, or less than the previous one. But the tonnage will definitely fall within one of these three options.

Yoshio Okawara, Japanese ambassador to Australia, on the beef quota, 1977

All I was doing was appealing for an endorsement, not suggesting you endorse it.

George Bush, to Colorado governor, campaign, 1992

We will not be abolishing the right to buy schooling: it is just that they [parents] will have to buy it abroad.

Neil Kinnock, on Labour's policy to abolish fee-charging for schooling, general election, 1983

The growth of post neo-classical endogenous growth theory and the symbiotic relationships between growth and investment.

Gordon Brown, shadow Chancellor, 1994

Job insecurity is a state of mind.

Ian Lang, President of the Board of Trade, November 1995

Democracy is more important than having a parliament.

Dr Peter Onu, acting Secretary-General of the Organization of African Unity, 1985

With these few words I want to assure you that I love you and if you had been a woman I would have considered marrying you, although your head is full of grey hairs, but as you are a man that possibility doesn't arise.

Ugandan President **Idi Amin** in a letter to Tanzanian President Nyerere, 1972

That canard was introduced as a red herring.

Former Jamaican Prime Minister **Michael Manley**, interview BBC World
Service, 1983

Our Cabinet is always unanimous – except when we disagree.

William Vander Zalm, Premier of British Columbia, Canada.

We are doing everything we would normally be doing, but more of it.

Israeli military spokesman seeking to play down the army's state of alert,
Jerusalem, October 1990

The Kurds who are being executed do not belong to the Kurdish people.

Ayatollah Khomeini, Iranian spiritual leader

I intend to open the country up to democracy, and anyone who is
against that I will jail, I will crush.

President João Figueiredo of Brazil, on his inauguration, 1979

Carter apparently doesn't even know that Michigan is one of the forty-
eight states.

Gerald Ford, campaigning for Ronald Reagan, 1980. Told there were fifty,
he recovered: 'I voted for Hawaii and Alaska [to become states] and I'm
proud of it.'

When Japan tells us 'yes', often it means 'no'. It is very important for the Japanese not to behave the same to you.

Boris Yeltsin advising Bill Clinton during US–Russian summit, Vancouver, April 1993. The White House later clarified the remarks as being 'casual comments about Japanese courtesy and etiquette'

No.

Tohei Kono, Japanese government spokesman, asked whether Japanese often mean 'no' when they say 'yes', April 1993

Following a nuclear attack on the United States, the United States Postal Service plans to distribute Emergency Change of Address Cards.

Executive Order 11490, US Federal Emergency Management Agency, 1969

It contains a misleading impression, not a lie. It was being economical with the truth.

Sir Robert Armstrong, Cabinet Secretary and head of the Civil Service, giving evidence in the *Spycatcher* trial, Sydney, November 1986

I have lied in good faith.

Bernard Tapie, former French minister, on trial for corruption, March 1995

We are, in a way, for Iraq and against Kuwait, and also for Kuwait and against Iraq.

Faisal Husseini, PLO spokesman, on Palestinian Gulf War loyalties, August 1990

I want blacks to feel that they are part of this country's existence. They are as much welcome at Buckingham Palace as anywhere else.
Prince Charles, 1982

We are sitting on a powder keg which could explode in our faces at any time.
Desmond Tutu, Archbishop of Cape Town, on the political situation in South Africa, 1985

It is a transparent smokescreen.
South African Conservative Party judgement on the government's plans for political reform, 1990

Sometimes you can have competing election promises.
Malcolm Fraser, future Australian Prime Minister, general election, 1976

We're part of a global world these days.
Brian Chamberlain, New Zealand agricultural trade special representative, 1990

We can beat the Liberals even with one engine tied behind our back.
Joe Clark, Conservative Prime Minister of Canada, 1979–80

A government is not an old pair of socks that you throw out. Come to think of it, you don't throw out old pairs of socks anyway these days.

Boris Yeltsin, Russian President, dismissing calls for his resignation, January 1992

The Israeli intelligence community is more open today than it has ever been. This is stated by a top military intelligence officer, Colonel 'A', who was speaking to our correspondent.

Israeli Defence Forces Radio, 1984

3 Shh!

Giving the Game Away

'Far better,' Norman Tebbit once snapped at an opponent, 'keep your mouth shut and let everyone think you're stupid, than open it and remove all doubt.' Cats out of bags – what the press call 'gaffes' – are often no more than flashes of lucidity, honesty or dangerous ambiguity. These can be fatal in public life. However tactless, those quoted below usually believed what they said. In some cases, they were horribly wrong, in others horribly right. A few would still stand by their remarks – and some may even be admired for their courage. But in most cases, it may be doubted (though not necessarily by them) whether they were wise to share their thoughts ...

A conservative government is an organized hypocrisy.

Benjamin Disraeli, future Conservative Prime Minister, opposing his own government on the Corn Laws, 1845

I never knew the lower classes had such white skins.

Alleged remark by **Lord Curzon**, member of the War Cabinet and former Viceroy of India, touring the Western Front during the First World War and seeing soldiers bathing

He is used to dealing with estate workers. I cannot see how anyone can say he is out of touch.

Lady Caroline Douglas-Home, Sir Alec's daughter, defending her father's credentials for the prime ministership, 1963

It is true that liberty is precious – so precious that it must be rationed.

Lenin (attr. by Sidney and Beatrice Webb, 1936)

A single death is a tragedy, a million deaths is a statistic.

Joseph Stalin

I admire Hitler because he pulled his country together when it was in a terrible state ... we need four or five Hitlers in Vietnam.

Nguyen Cao Ky, American-backed Premier of South Vietnam 1965–7

We are not without accomplishment. We have managed to distribute poverty equally.

Nguyen Co Thach, Foreign Minister, Communist Vietnam

All they want is a tight c**t, loose shoes and a warm place to shit.

Earl Butz, US Agriculture Secretary, campaigning for President Ford, questioned why his Republican Party had not recruited more blacks, 1976

We have every kind of mixture you can have. I have a black, I have a woman, two Jews and a cripple.

James Watt, US Interior Secretary, on the balanced composition of an advisory group, 1983. The remark cost him his job

If the criminal wants to commit suicide, then he should be allowed to do so. Something should be left in the cell. Perhaps a razor blade.

Jonathan Guinness, (unsuccessful) Conservative candidate, Lincoln by-election, 1973

Bunnies *can* and *will* go to France. In haste. Yours affectionately, Jeremy. PS. I miss you.

Letter from **Jeremy Thorpe** to sometime male model Norman Scott, 1961

People are really rather afraid that this country might be rather swamped by people with a different culture.

Margaret Thatcher, leader of the Opposition, 1978

I wouldn't say she was open minded on the Middle East so much as empty-headed. For instance, she probably thinks that Sinai is the plural of sinus.

Jonathan Aitken MP, on Margaret Thatcher during the party leadership election, 1975

Social security scroungers should be made to give a pint of blood every six months.

Michael Brotherton MP, 1979

He didn't riot. He got on his bike and looked for work.

Norman Tebbit, on his father's attitude to unemployment, Conservative Party conference, 1981

We can beat them in the 1980s and 1990s. We have beaten them in other respects and we can do it again.

John Butcher, junior trade and industry minister, on Japan, 1984

Bongo Bongo land.

Alan Clark, Employment Minister, referring to the origins of an African delegation, 1985

I spent lots of time with women ... I actually had sexual intercourse with some of them.

George Galloway MP, describing a charity conference in Greece, 1985. 'My sex orgy by MP' and 'I bonked for Britain' were the tabloid headlines.

It would be physically impossible ... a doctor can examine me if he wishes. These operations do work, don't they?

Ron Brown MP, denying reports that an alleged mistress was pregnant by him, 1988

There is nothing I can do for him professionally.

Mr Brown's fellow MP, **Sam Galbraith**, a brain surgeon

At least if I'd been f**king somebody I would have been having some fun.

Alan Duncan MP, commenting on being criticized for a property deal, 1994

The Cricket Test – which side do they cheer for?

Norman Tebbit, patriarch of the Conservative right, controversially introducing a new yardstick for successful racial integration, 1990

A German racket to take over the whole of Europe. It has to be thwarted.

Nicholas Ridley, Trade and Industry Secretary, on European monetary union, interview in the *Spectator*, 1990. He resigned within days

Speeches that somebody delivered on a wet night in Dudley.

Kenneth Clarke, Chancellor of the Exchequer, telling the party conference that these did not (unlike manifesto pledges) count as 'commitments', 1993

When I hear the name Richard Body, I hear the sound of white coats flapping.

John Major, on one of his own MPs, 1994 (attrib.)

Bastards

Major, caught off-guard describing the Euro-sceptics in his party, 1994

They are all the same. They're short, they're fat and they are fundamentally corrupt.

Rod Richards, junior Welsh Office minister, on Welsh Labour councillors, 1995

I wish that cow would resign.

Richard Needham, Northern Ireland Minister, on his car telephone to his wife, airing his views on the Prime Minister, 1990. The call was overheard and recorded by a radio eavesdropper. (He later telephoned Mrs Thatcher and apologized.)

If any of you have got an A-level, it is because you have worked to get it. Go to any other country and when you have got an A-level, you have bought it.

Michael Portillo, Chief Secretary to the Treasury, speech to students at Southampton University, February 1994

Imagine – the European Commission might want to harmonize uniforms and cap badges, or even metricate them. The European Court would probably want to stop our men fighting for more than forty hours a week. They would send half of them home on paternity leave.

Portillo, now Defence Secretary, Conservative Party conference, October 1995

In exceptional cases it is necessary to say something that is untrue to the House of Commons. The House of Commons understands that and has always accepted that.

William Waldegrave, Minister for Open Government, appearing before a Commons select committee, declaring that ministers were sometimes entitled to lie to Parliament, March 1994

There's a lot that can be done in terms of encouraging more people to enjoy a cheap and cheerful service at one moment in the day for the typists and perhaps a more luxurious service for the civil servants and businessmen who might travel at a slightly different time.

Roger Freeman, public transport minister, infuriating secretaries, 1992

You have your own company, your own temperature control, your own music and you don't have to put up with dreadful human beings sitting alongside you.

Steven Norris, Minister of Transport, favouring the private car over public transport, February 1995

I must remember to declare it in the Register of Interests.

Conservative Minister **Neil Hamilton**, brandishing a biscuit after a factory visit. He had been criticized for alleged failure to declare interests. This gaffe (as it was seen) helped seal his fate as a minister, 1994.

Crikey!

Norman Fowler, Health Secretary, wiping his brow when a civil servant, advising on the spread of Aids, explained to him what oral sex was (attrib.)

[You have] to use the resources you've got to make any occupation totally untenable.

Neil Kinnock, explaining Labour's defence policy during general election campaign, 1987, widely interpreted as contemplating invasion of Britain and a guerrilla warfare strategy

If we had the death penalty, [they] would have been forgotten [and] we shouldn't have had all these campaigns to get them released.

Lord Denning, former Master of the Rolls, August 1990, on the case of the Birmingham Six, jailed for life in 1975 for allegedly being responsible for an IRA bombing in the city. They were released in 1991 after the verdicts were declared unsafe by the Appeal Court

We should not be cowards … maybe that includes taxing and selling cannabis.

Clare Short, Labour frontbencher, October 1995

The party has a clear position against legalizing soft drugs and I am perfectly happy with it.

Short, the next day

I think in a fair tax system, people like me would pay a bit more tax.

Clare Short, April 1996

It would be mischievous to see my remark as a call for higher taxes for people on middle incomes.

Short, 'clarifying' statement issued later same day.

I will not be silenced.

Short, the next day

We go to the shadow Cabinet. We go to the National Executive Committee. Everything we do is in the light. They live in the dark. It is a good place for them.

Clare Short on her party leader's advisers, whom she described as 'dark forces', August 1996

I can't think of any major policy differences between the three of us.

Tony Blair on himself, and leadership rivals Margaret Beckett and John Prescott, BBC TV, 12 June 1994

I had quite fundamental disagreements with Tony.

John Prescott, 25 June 1994

The Balkanization of Britain ... Pimply politics.

Kim Howells, Labour frontbencher, on Welsh devolution

[Liberal Democrat] policies are so expensive they would bankrupt the nation X number of times.

[Liberal Democrat] policy on fundholding GPs is, at best, confused and at worst, duplicitous.

Lib-Dems will cripple the economy by buying back Railtrack. They are anti-road barmies.

Lib-Dems say everything to everybody.

Extracts from a leaked Liberal Democrat document describing the appearance of their policies in the eyes of some voters, January 1996. 'Obviously this document will have a very limited circulation,' the anonymous author said.

Mrs Thatcher will go down as one of the great Prime Ministers of this country.

Paddy Ashdown, Liberal Democrat leader, 1988

They lack fragrance on the whole. They're definitely not desert island material ... They all look as though they are from the 5th Kiev Stalinist machine-gun parade.

Sir Nicholas Fairbairn, deprecating the lack of style of women MPs

What's a skirt but an open gateway?

Fairbairn

The TUC is not involved in party politics. Nor is its General Secretary ... I hope that every trade unionist with a vote in Walsall, Workington and Newcastle will cast it next Thursday for the Labour candidate.

TUC General Secretary, **Len Murray**, before three by-elections, 1976

Liberty is conforming to the majority.

Hugh Scanlon, Engineering Workers' union leader, 1977

The Russians are praying for a Labour victory.

Denis Healey, Labour foreign affairs spokesman, opening day of the general election campaign, 1987

If you vote for Kinnock, you are voting against Christ.

Dame Barbara Cartland, campaign, 1992

This union has had as much effect on wages as breaking wind has on the Richter scale.

Delegate to the National Union of Mineworkers' conference, 1988

Many immigrants vote Labour because they think the labour exchanges where they sign on for unemployment benefit belong to the Labour Party.

Dharam Duggal, ward chairman, Birmingham Conservative Association, quoted *Sunday Times, c* 1980

F**k off out of it if you can't observe the niceties.

Robert McCartney, Unionist member of the Ulster Assembly, to an English journalist not standing for the singing of the national anthem, November 1984

We must be mad, literally mad, as a nation to be permitting the annual inflow of some 50,000 dependants of immigrants … As I look ahead I am filled with foreboding. Like the Roman, I see the River Tiber foaming with much blood.

Enoch Powell, Conservative shadow defence spokesman, exiting from mainstream British politics, 1968

I don't really think I have ever made a mistake.

Powell, *Any Questions?*, BBC Radio, 1982

To assume that because a party has one dominant figure it thereby benefits is not necessarily true at all. ... Nobody expects that the Prime Minister would be Prime Minister throughout the entire period of the next Parliament.

John Biffen, Leader of the House, curtailing his political career, interview on *Weekend World* (ITV), May 1986. In the same interview, he described his hopes that the Tory leadership at the next election would be 'a balanced ticket'. It sparked a furious, although indirect, response from Mrs Thatcher who let it be known through her press secretary that she regarded Biffen as a 'semi-detached' member of the government. He was sacked two days after the general election in 1987

Our human stock is threatened. ... These mothers ... single parents from classes 4 and 5 are now producing a third of all births. If we do nothing, the nation moves towards degeneration.

Sir Keith Joseph speaking to Birmingham Conservatives, October 1974. He went on to recommend 'proposals to extend birth control to these classes of people'. Reaction ended his hopes of leading his party, clearing the way for Margaret Thatcher in 1975.

Conservatism, like selfishness, is inherent in the human condition.

Sir Keith Joseph, *New Statesman*, 1975

The price of oil is not determined by the British Parliament. It is determined by some lads riding camels who do not even know how to spell national sovereignty.

Lord Feather, former TUC General Secretary, 1975

It was easier for a camel to go through the eye of a needle than for a rich man to get into the Kingdom of Heaven, so if the rich are taxed more heavily at least it would be partially for their own good.

Ivor Clemitson MP, 1975

I will consider selling off the Crown Jewels – but I am not absolutely certain that they are the property of Her Majesty's Government.

Denis Healey, Chancellor of the Exchequer, in the year Britain was bailed out by the IMF, 1976

That's OK, we milk the public for a living.

Unidentified MP on a 'fact-finding' visit to the United States in 1991 replying off the cuff to a Hudson, Wisconsin farmer Vernon Bailey, who had introduced himself by saying, 'I milk cows for a living.' The party included Tories Roger King, James Cran and Andrew Hargreaves, and Labour's Tom Pendry and Allen McKay, but the perpetrator was not identified.

I have difficulty looking humble for extended periods of time.

Henry Kissinger, 1981

I am being frank about myself in this book. I tell of my first mistake on page 850.

Kissinger, on his memoirs, *The White House Years*, 1979

The longer I am out of office, the more infallible I appear to myself.

Kissinger

The nice thing about being a celebrity is that when you bore people, they think it's their fault.

Kissinger, 1985

I don't give a damn about protocol. I'm a swinger. Bring out the beautiful spies.

Kissinger, reacting to seating plans for an official dinner, 1973

He doesn't make snap decisions, but he doesn't overthink either.

Nancy Reagan, on Ronald, 1980

I'm not doing so bad. At this point in his administration, William Henry Harrison had been dead sixty-eight days.

President Clinton, four months after his inauguration, after a series of public relations disasters in making appointments to his administration, May 1993

I'm a great believer in leaving politics when you've reached your ceiling. (*Pause*) Though, I did lower the ceiling somewhat ...

Cecil Parkinson, former cabinet minister, on leaving the Commons, campaign 1992

Other than when playing darts, I become confused at the mere mention of figures.

Neil Kinnock, then a Labour backbencher, House of Commons 1978. (The following year, he became the party's chief spokesman on education.)

I wonder how it is with you, Harold? If I don't have a woman for three days, I get a terrible headache.

President John Kennedy to Prime Minister Harold Macmillan, during working lunch on nuclear arms, 1962

I usually make up my mind about a man in ten seconds, and I very rarely change it.

Margaret Thatcher, Education Secretary, 1970

Oh Lord, teach me to learn that occasionally I make mistakes.

Thatcher, quoting her favourite poem, *Today*, BBC Radio, 1982

It is exciting to have a real crisis on your hands when you have spent half your life dealing with humdrum issues like the environment.

Thatcher, speech to the Scottish Conservative conference, May 1982, during the Falklands war

I've looked on a lot of women with lust. I've committed adultery in my heart many times.

Jimmy Carter, *Playboy* interview, campaign 1976

If I'd known that Enrique was going to be President of Bolivia, I'd have sent him to school.

A nineteenth-century Bolivian President's mother

You know, the main shortcoming of all socialist countries is that we are not clever with figures.

Kim Dal Hyon, deputy Prime Minister of North Korea, asked how much the government had spent celebrating the eightieth birthday of dictator Kim Il Sung, May 1992

Among some people in this country, for a man to express his love for his wife he must beat her sometimes.

George Mashamba, South African senator, addressing a parliamentary committee on education, September 1995

Leave it where you got it.

Terry Troutt, Mayor of Romulus, Michigan, public announcement to anyone 'with a body on their hands', after complaining that his town just outside Detroit was being used as a dumping ground by murderers, 1973

Ah, so next time we shall not be able to hear them coming.

Pierre Mendes-France, former French Prime Minister, undiplomatic slip in response to news that German soldiers' jackboots were now fitted with rubber soles, 1960

You need to put your ideas down where the goats can get them.

Governor **George Wallace**'s advice on projecting policies in simple ways that voters can grasp, quoted during presidential election campaign, 1988

The majority of those men are homosexual – perhaps not the majority – but in the USA there are already 25 per cent of them and in England and Germany it is the same. You cannot imagine it in the history of France.

Edith Cresson, French Prime Minister, 1991 (attrib.)

They sit up all night thinking of ways to screw the Americans and the Europeans.

Cresson, on the Japanese economic threat, 1991

I don't see this as an undesirable phenomenon. On the contrary, some-times it's good to let out your fury, as long as it is within the bounds of reason.

Ehud Kinamon, Mayor of the Israeli town of Bat Yam, after four nights of rioting by townspeople following the stabbing of an Israeli by a Palestinian, June 1992

We're in a battle that is like searching for a needle in a haystack. Sometimes to find the needle you need to burn the whole haystack.

Ezer Weizman, Israeli President, March 1996

Where would Christianity be if Jesus had got eight to fifteen years with time off for good behaviour?

James Donovan, New York senator supporting capital punishment, 1978

What would we do? ... It might end with a Cuba off our western coast.

James Prior, Northern Ireland Secretary, on the prospect of Sinn Fein nationalists winning more seats than moderates in future Ulster elections, November 1983

If you've seen one city slum, you've seen them all.

Spiro Agnew, campaigning as Richard Nixon's vice-presidential running mate, Detroit, 1968

A tree's a tree. How many do you need to look at?

Ronald Reagan, on plans to expand California's Redwood National Park, 1967

Seen one Redwood, you've seen 'em all.

Reagan on ecology, quoted Melbourne *Age*, 1981

Why should we subsidize intellectual curiosity?

Reagan, opposing increased education spending

If it takes a bloodbath, let's get it over with. No more appeasement.

Reagan, when Governor of California, on police action against student anti-war demonstrators, 1970

We've got to pause and ask ourselves: How much clean air do we need?

Lee Iacocca, chairman of the Chrysler Corporation, responding to tougher environmental laws on vehicle emissions

Boy, they were big on crematoriums, weren't they?

George Bush, Vice-President, after visiting the death camp at Auschwitz, 1987

The B-52 has been an effective war machine. It's killed a lot of people.

Bill Young, speaking on the floor of the US House of Representatives

The B-52 has been an effective war machine which unfortunately has killed a lot of people.

Young as recorded in the Congressional Record after 'sanitizing' his speech. Quoted Melbourne *Age*, 1981

I want to lob one into the men's room of the Kremlin and to make sure I hit it.

Barry Goldwater, Republican presidential candidate against Lyndon Johnson, on his ambitions for nuclear weapons, campaign 1964

I wanted to educate the American people to lose some of their fear of the word 'nuclear'. When you say 'nuclear', all the American people see is a mushroom cloud. But for military purposes, it's just enough firepower to get the job done.

Goldwater, responding to criticism of his recklessness, 1964

I haven't got a really first-class brain.

Goldwater, campaign 1964

If we have to start over again with another Adam and Eve, I want them to be Americans and not Russians.

Richard Russell, US senator for Georgia, 1968

In the Orient, life is cheap.

General William Westmoreland, commander-in-chief of US troops in Vietnam, *c* 1967

We should declare war on North Vietnam. We could pave the whole country and put parking stripes on it, and still be home by Christmas.

Ronald Reagan, when Governor of California, 1966

If we quit Vietnam, tomorrow we'll be fighting in Hawaii and next week we'll have to fight in San Francisco.

Lyndon Johnson, 1967

If only Hitler and Mussolini could have a good game of bowls once a week at Geneva, I feel that Europe would not be as troubled as it is.

Capt R G Briscoe MP, *c* 1937

I often think how much easier the world would have been to manage if Herr Hitler and Signor Mussolini had been at Oxford.

Lord Halifax, Foreign Secretary, 1938–41

Are you aware it is private property? Why you'll be asking me to bomb Essen next.

Sir Kingsley Wood, Secretary of State for Air, on plans to set fire to the
Black Forest, September 1939

If America does not watch out, it will be judged as finished by the world. [America has become] Japan's sub-contractor.

Yoshio Sakurauchi, Speaker of Japan's House of Representatives, claiming
that America's trade imbalance with Japan was due to laziness and illiteracy
among US workers, January 1992

[My remarks were] short of explanation and liable to cause misunderstanding.

Sakurauchi, apologizing the next day

I was greatly moved to see how much the American workers want to make high-efficiency, high-quality products. Even more than the Japanese employees you'd see in a plant in Japan, the Americans working in a Toyota or Honda plant in America have a way of working that is just splendid.

Kabun Muto, newly appointed Japanese Foreign Minister, sent to repair
Japanese–American relations, April 1993

I read about foreign policy and studied – I know the number of continents.

George Wallace, presidential candidate, campaigning 1968

Well, I never saw this before. I didn't write this speech and don't believe what I just read.

Warren Harding, stumbling over speech, campaign trail, 1920. (He won in a landslide.)

Something's going awry here. I mean, if I just listen to the question, I can answer whatever it is. But if it's going to be on [the script] I don't listen to the question, I just look at [the script].

George Bush, on an open microphone, inadvertently revealing that supposedly spontaneous questions from an audience, the answers to which were displayed on a teleprompter, were not coming in the order scripted by his staff, November 1991

I will learn as I go along.

William Clark, Ronald Reagan's choice as Deputy Secretary of State, who revealed in his nomination hearings in 1981 that he didn't know the names of the South African or Zimbabwean leaders, had not heard of the split in the British Labour Party, had 'no opinion' on the spread of nuclear weapons and relied solely on news magazines for his understanding of foreign affairs

Ireland has food and climate well matched for each other: dull.

The private observations of diplomat **Robin Berrington**, Cultural Affairs and Press Officer at the American Embassy in Dublin, mistakenly included in the Embassy's publicity handout marking President Reagan's inauguration, 1981

Pretty small potatoes compared to the other countries of Europe.

Ditto

While Ireland is undoubtedly a great place to visit, living and working here is something else.

Ditto

I came to gain a greater appreciation of the similarities and differences between the inscrutable Irish and the insufferable English.

Ditto

The Irish are famous for their sense of humour. I think I shall have to rely upon it in this instance.

Berrington's boss, **Ambassador William Shannon**, smoothing the ruffled feathers.

Journalist: Are you not worn out by all the late nights?
Lord Halifax: Not exactly, but it spoils one's eye for the high birds.

Exchange immediately after the Munich crisis, October 1938

I am sure I will feel at home in the Bahamas ... I love golf and they have a lot of nice golf courses and good fishing.

Chic Hecht, Bush's nominee for US ambassador to the Bahamas, 1989. He was appointed

I saw the new Italian navy. Its boats have glass bottoms so they can see the old Italian navy.

Peter Secchia, President Bush's nominee for US ambassador to Italy, during Senate confirmation hearings, 1989. He too was approved

If the B-2 is invisible, just announce you've built a hundred of them and don't build them.

John Kasich, chairman US House Budget Committee, opposing further expenditure on the Stealth bomber designed to be invisible to radar detection, July 1995

If we [legislators] don't watch our respective tails, the people are going to be running the government.

Bill Craven, Californian state senator, on the growing use of citizen-inspired state referendums

Let [the French and the Germans] put their demands in such a way that Great Britain can say that she supported both sides.

Ramsay MacDonald, Prime Minister, minutes of the Five Power conference in Geneva on disarmament and security in Europe, December 1932

It is better to do something quite absurd for which there is a precedent than to make oneself responsible for an unprecedented act of wisdom.

Arthur Balfour, Foreign Secretary, defending the traditions of secret diplomacy in response to the call for 'open' diplomacy in American President Woodrow Wilson's Fourteen Points, House of Commons, 1918

I retract any statement that might have created the impression that any individual should be targeted for physical attack.

Peter Mokaba, South African ANC youth leader, clarifying his remarks after he had urged township residents to 'save their bullets' for President F W de Klerk, August 1993

The chap's got no experience of government. He's hardly made a speech, or held a press conference. (*Pause*) Mind you, I suppose it's not entirely his fault.

Pik Botha, South African Foreign Minister, on the credentials for leadership of the then still jailed Nelson Mandela, reported by David Steel MP during visit, 1986

In Israel, in order to be realistic, you have to believe in miracles.

David Ben-Gurion, first Prime Minister of Israel

Marijuana smokers, drug addicts, long-hairs, homosexuals and unionists.

General Pinochet, former President of Chile, describing the West German army, 1990. He later issued an apology saying that his comments 'were never meant to offend the army'

If you want to steal, steal a little cleverly, in a nice way. If you steal so much as to become rich overnight, you will be caught.

Mobutu Sese Seko, President of Zaire, anti-corruption speech 1976. His own fortune plundered from his country is estimated at $5 billion

If they managed to build the Hilton in the middle of Brixton, I promise I would stay there.

Al Sharpton, US black political activist, on a visit to London 'to denounce British racism' on the reason for staying at a £300-a-night hotel in London's exclusive Mayfair, May 1991

From 20,000 feet in the air, on the way to Paris.

Australian Prime Minister **Paul Keating**, when asked the best way to see Darwin, the Northern Territory port, quoted 1996

Bribe expenses are tax deductible, provided companies can document that they were necessary to secure a sale of goods or a business contract.

Ole Stavad, Danish tax minister, June 1993

I was thinking of you last night, Helmut, because I was watching the sumo wrestling on television.

Bill Clinton, greeting Germany's Chancellor Kohl, at NATO summit, Brussels, January 1994

We have that trouble in our family, too.

Prince Philip, during a visit to Australia, 1954, being introduced to a married couple. The husband had introduced them by saying, 'My wife's a doctor of philosophy. She is much more important than me.'

Wasn't it too bad you sent your royal family to the guillotine?

Prince Philip, to the French Minister of the Interior, on the tumultuous reception he and Queen Elizabeth received from Parisian crowds during their visit, April 1957

I never see any home cooking – all I get is fancy stuff.

Prince Philip, 1962

Are you sure you want to go through with this?

Prince Philip, aside to new Prime Minister Jomo Kenyatta during the Kenya independence ceremony in 1963, inadvertently picked up by microphones and broadcast to the watching crowd

The monarchy exists not for its own benefit, but for that of the country. We don't come here for our health. We can think of better ways of enjoying ourselves.

Prince Philip, addressing audience in Ottawa, royal visit to Canada

What a po-faced lot these Dutch are.

Prince Philip, during motorcade drive on visit to Amsterdam, 1968

Five per cent! Five per cent! You must be out of your minds.

Prince Philip, on learning the birthrate on a visit to the Solomon Islands, 1982

Don't stay here too long or you'll go back with slitty eyes.

Prince Philip, to British students in Peking, 1986

Manchester is not such a nice place.

Queen Elizabeth, to a student in St Petersburg, 1994

A few years ago everybody was saying we must have more leisure, everybody is working too much. Now that everybody has got so much leisure – it may be involuntary, but they have got it – they are now complaining they are unemployed. People do not seem to be able to make up their minds, do they?

Prince Philip, 1981

I'm prepared to take advice on leisure from Prince Philip. He's a world expert on leisure. He's been practising for most of his adult life.

Neil Kinnock

The grouse are in no danger from those who shoot grouse.

Prince Philip, on conservationist approaches to field sports, 1988

I don't think a prostitute is more moral than a wife, but they are doing the same thing.

Prince Philip, 1988

How do you keep the natives off the booze long enough to get them past the test?

Prince Philip, to a driving instructor during a visit to Oban, 1995

It makes me look so old, but then I suppose I am old.

Queen Elizabeth, on newly designed £5 notes which showed her with a double chin, wrinkles and bags under her eyes, June 1990

The monarchy is the oldest profession in the world.

Prince Charles, *c* 1980 (attrb.)

My favourite programme is *Mrs Dale's Diary*. I try never to miss it because it is the only way of knowing what goes on in the middle-class family.

Queen Elizabeth the Queen Mother: the radio serial ran from 1948 to 1969

Just call me Madam.

Betty Boothroyd, first woman Deputy Speaker of the Commons, advising MPs how to address her, 1987

She is vulgar, vulgar, vulgar.

Martin Charteris, private secretary in the Royal household, leaked opinion on the Duchess of York

This woman is headstrong, obstinate and dangerously self-opinionated.

Report by personnel office at ICI, rejecting the 22-year-old Margaret Roberts (soon-to-be Thatcher) as a possible employee, 1948

SITUATIONS: DOMESTIC. Cheerful, energetic and loving nanny/ mother's help [who could] enjoy the relaxed and happy life in our family with Amy, 3, Hanna, 5, Lizzi, 10, and Nicky, 12.

Advertisement placed in *The Lady* magazine for June 1984 by a lady who turned out to be Councillor Mrs Margaret Hodge, then Leader of the red-flag-flying and Lenin's-bust-displaying Islington Borough Council and now Labour frontbencher and MP for Barking. The advertisement added that a cleaner was also employed and there were 'plenty of local nannies'.

4   *Er ...*

If Only They'd Known

New facts can be inconvenient and the march of history can be straight over one's blithest assumptions. Events can leave politicians floundering, but the statesman who never said anything the passage of time left him regretting, never said anything. Those quoted below were bolder, worse luck. 'If I knew then what I know now ... '

The French people are incapable of regicide.

Louis XVI of France, four years before he was guillotined, 1789

A difficult and hardly comprehensible work which few would read and still fewer understand.

Russian official censor, 1881, passing Marx's *Das Kapital* for translation into Russian, quoted by David McLellan, *Karl Marx: The Legacy*, 1983

The day of the small nations has long passed away. The day of Empires has come.

Joseph Chamberlain, former colonial secretary, speech, 1904

England is at last ripe for revolution.

Leon Trotsky, 1925

He falls instantly in and out of love. His present attachment will follow the course of all the others.

Winston Churchill, on Edward VIII's relationship with Mrs Simpson, 1936

The men who win wars are the men with burning hearts and cool heads ... It is because I see that combination present in the Prime Minister that I would rather trust him to lead us to victory than any other man.

Henry Brooke MP, consigning himself to backbench obscurity by supporting Neville Chamberlain in the famous Commons debate of 1940 which led to Chamberlain's resignation and Churchill's premiership. Brooke had to wait fourteen years for his first ministerial post; he rose to be Home Secretary, 1962–4

It is certain as the day that a Labour town council, a Socialist or Communist government, would not for a day tolerate strikes in social or other services necessary for the life of the nation.

George Lansbury, Labour Party leader, 1934

No evidence has been found to show that [Kim Philby] was responsible for warning Burgess or Maclean. While in government service he carried out his duties ably and conscientiously. I have no reason to conclude that Mr Philby has at any time betrayed the interests of this country, or to identify him with the so-called 'third man', if, indeed, there was one.

Harold Macmillan, then Foreign Secretary, House of Commons debate on the defection of Soviet spies Burgess and Maclean, November 1955

[The security services] are now aware ... that he worked for the Soviet authorities before 1946 and that in 1951 he in fact warned Maclean through Burgess that the security services were about to take action against him.

Edward Heath, Lord Privy Seal, statement to the House, July 1963

If the British public falls for this, I say it will be stark staring bonkers.

Quintin Hogg (Lord Hailsham), on the Labour election manifesto, 1964. (It did.)

If I were a football manager, on present form I would be more worried about job security than I am as Prime Minister.

Harold Wilson, April 1970. (Two months later he fell from office in one of the least expected electoral upsets of the century.)

Our problem at the moment is a problem of success.

Edward Heath, a month and a half before the three-day week, November 1973

I am not proposing to seek your votes because there is blue sky ahead today.

James Callaghan, Prime Minister, broadcast to the nation, announcing his decision not to call a general election, September 1978. The Winter of Discontent which followed put paid to his chances of re-election when the election did come the following May.

When calm returns to the industrial scene, this week's agreement between the Government and the TUC will prove to be a major turning point, which will provide the basis for a great Labour victory at the general election.

Joel Barnett, Chief Secretary to the Treasury, on Labour's agreement ending the Winter of Discontent, February 1979. They lost to Mrs Thatcher in the general election three months later

To my mind, the only give and take in the social contract was that the government gave and the unions took.

Barnett, February 1982

The Tories are now conscious that they have lost the fight for public support.

Robin Cook, on the Government's nuclear weapons policy, *Labour Herald*, October 1981

The forthcoming general election will be the most open battle in recent political history.

Roy Hattersley, Labour shadow home affairs spokesman, March 1983. The election in June resulted in a 144 seat Conservative majority, the biggest since 1945. By contrast, Labour won the lowest ever share of the vote by a principal party of opposition

We will govern as we have campaigned – strongly, positively, looking to the future. The contrast with the Tories could not be more sharp. They are a spent force.

Neil Kinnock, party election rally, Sheffield, 1992

We're all right. We're all right. We're all right. We're all right.

Kinnock, Sheffield, 1992, days before losing

I plan to be the Gromyko of the Labour Party for the next thirty years.

Denis Healey, Labour shadow foreign affairs spokesman, 1984, after the change of party leader, aiming to emulate the Soviet Foreign Minister (1957–85) and later President (1985–8), who served under five Soviet leaders. However, he decided not to contest his seat at the 1992 general election.

Go back to your constituencies and prepare for government!

David Steel, Liberal leader to Liberal Party conference, 1985

I sense that the British electorate is now itching to break out once and for all from the discredited strait-jacket of the past.

Steel, general election, June 1987. The itch was contained

We witness on every hand unchallenged male dominance, arrogant armaments, harsh and unfeeling administration of the law. With the incoming of the mother element into politics this would be gradually changed.

Keir Hardie, Labour Party pioneer, foreseeing a kinder, gentler politics if women became involved, 1907

Yesterday was hers; tomorrow is ours.

Neil Kinnock, Labour Party leader, on Mrs Thatcher's tenth anniversary in power, May 1989

She'll be Prime Minister until the middle of the next century.

Jeffrey Archer, on Margaret Thatcher, 1989

We are definitely in for the last few weeks of Thatcherism – the last few weeks of that job-destroying, oil-wasting, truth-twisting, service-smashing, nation-splitting bunch of twisters under a one-person government.

Neil Kinnock, Labour leader in overdrive, general election, 1987. (He lost to a Conservative landslide.)

This is only the third time of asking. I hope to go on and on.

Margaret Thatcher, general election campaign, 1987

The Chancellor's position is unassailable.

Thatcher endorsing Nigel Lawson, shortly before she began to assail it herself by taking separate economic advice from her personal adviser Sir Alan Walters. Lawson resigned in protest in 1989 after she refused his ultimatum to dismiss Walters.

He will never get to the top in English [*sic*] politics, for all his wonderful gifts; to speak with the tongue of men and angels, and to spend laborious days and nights in administration is not good if a man does not inspire trust.

Herbert Asquith, on Winston Churchill

His style ... is not very literary, and he lacks force.

Daily News, reporting Winston Churchill's maiden speech in the House of Commons, February 1901

If paternity leave was granted, it would result in a direct incitement to a population explosion.

Ian Gow MP, 1979

By the end of 1991, it is not unreasonable to suppose that motoring will become an occupation indulged in by the super rich, just as it was in the early 1920s.

Lord Tanlaw, Liberal peer, 1977

If cars continue to be made at the same rate as now and with increasing cheapness, there will soon be no pedestrians left.

Leslie Hore-Belisha, Minister of Transport, 1935

Personally, I do not believe that we shall have greater armaments in the future than we have had in the past. On the contrary, I believe there will be a gradual diminution in this respect.

William Watson, MP, House of Commons, 1924

[The atomic bomb] is the biggest fool thing we have ever done ... The bomb will never go off – and I speak as an expert in explosives.

Admiral William Leahy, US chief of staff advising President Truman, 1945

Atomic energy might be as good as our present day explosives, but it is unlikely to produce anything very much more dangerous.

Winston Churchill, 1939

The Olympic movement appears as a ray of sunshine through the clouds of racial animosity, religious bigotry and political chicanery.

Avery Brundage, President of the International Olympic Committee, 1972, before the Munich massacre, the Montreal games which were boycotted by the Africans, the Moscow games which were boycotted by the West, and the Los Angeles games which were boycotted by the Eastern bloc

It could no more lose money than I could have a baby.

Jean Drapeau, Mayor of Montreal, on his city hosting the 1976 Olympics, January 1973. The games left Montreal with a debt of over $1 billion.

It has become apparent ... that any attempt to retain the present building, even with such modernization as would be possible structurally, would be uneconomic and would fail to provide accommodation suitable for present-day conditions, let alone future requirements.

Geoffrey Rippon, Minister of Public Building and Works, announcing his decision to demolish the mid-nineteenth century Foreign Office building and build a modern replacement, November 1963. (Although the decision had the support of the Labour opposition, the plans were shelved when Harold Wilson came to power the following year.)

There will be one million AIDS cases in Britain by the end of 1991.

World Health Organization report, July 1989. By March 1994 there had been just 9,000 cases

Within a decade we will build a world party of socialist revolution [and become] the decisive force on the planet.

Militant Tendency publicity, 1981

We in America today are nearer to the final triumph over poverty than ever before in the history of any land ... We shall soon with the help of God be in sight of the day when poverty will be banished from this nation.

Herbert Hoover, soon-to-be President, accepting the Republican nomination, 1928, twelve months before the Great Crash

No Congress of the United States ever assembled, on surveying the state of the Union, has met with a more pleasing prospect than that which appears at the present time.

Calvin Coolidge, December 1928

The government's business is in sound condition.

Andrew Mellon, US Secretary of the Treasury, five weeks after the crash, December 1929

I see nothing ... in the present situation that is either menacing or warrants pessimism.

Mellon, January 1930

The worst effect of the crash upon unemployment will have been passed during the next sixty days.

President Hoover, March 1930. Unemployment was then some three million. It reached thirteen million, at the end of 1932, before recovery began

We are likely to find the country as a whole enjoying its wonted state of prosperity. Business will be normal in two months.

Robert Lamont, Secretary of Commerce, March 1930

Normal conditions should be restored in two or three months.

Lamont, May 1930

The worst is over without a doubt.

James Davis, US Agriculture Secretary, six months into the Great Depression, June 1930

Courage and resource are already swinging us back on the road to recovery.

Davis, six weeks later

We have hit bottom and are on the upswing.

Davis, September 1930

The decline in business has substantially if not wholly ceased.

Robert Lamont, Secretary of Commerce, September 1930

There undoubtedly will be an appreciable decrease in the number of unemployed by mid-summer.

Lamont, March 1931

The green shoots of economic spring are appearing once again.

Norman Lamont, Chancellor of the Exchequer, House of Commons, October 1991

I have been singing in the bath.

Lamont, at the Munich G7 economic summit, July 1992, two months before he withdrew Britain from the European Exchange Rate Mechanism

Je ne regrette rien.

Lamont, May 1993, replying to a TV interviewer during the Newbury by-election campaign, which the Conservatives lost

In all likelihood, world inflation is over.

Per Jacobsson, managing director of the International Monetary Fund, 1959

It is doubtful ... if German production would be such as to challenge our strong position in most markets outside Europe.

Conclusion of report on Britain's export outlook, Board of Trade, 1950

You can forget about OPEC [the organization of oil-producing countries]. They will never amount to a row of beans.

Lord Robens, Chairman of the National Coal Board 1961–71, quoting the advice he received from a senior Ministry of Power official in 1967

We are facing a new era. Labour can deliver the goods.

Clement Attlee, on becoming Prime Minister, 1945

We have turned our backs on the economics of scarcity.

Herbert Morrison, deputy Prime Minister, Labour Party conference, 1946

I have no easy words for the nation. I cannot say when we shall emerge into easier times.

Clement Attlee, introducing emergency austerity measures during the economic crisis, 1947

I sum up the prospects for 1967 in three short sentences. We are back on course. The ship is picking up speed. The economy is moving. Every seaman knows the command at such a moment, 'Steady as she goes.'

James Callaghan, Chancellor of the Exchequer, Budget speech, March 1967. By the autumn, he had to recommend devaluation of the pound by 14 per cent.

We thought we could put the economy right in five years. We were wrong. It will probably take ten.

Tony Benn, 1968

Conservatives should welcome controls on prices and incomes, even as a permanent feature of the economy.

John Major, before election as an MP, Conservative constituency meeting, February 1973

The community charge is the most potent weapon ever put in the hands of ordinary voters to defeat incompetent and malign Labour councils ... Far from being a vote loser, with your help it will be a vote winner and launch us on our fourth term.

Michael Portillo, then local government minister, defending the poll tax as a 'vote winner', Conservative Party conference, October 1990

We stand for a country united around those old common sense values that should never have been pushed aside.

John Major, 'Back to Basics' party conference speech 1993

It is in everyone's interests to reduce broken families and the number of single parents; I have seen from my constituency the consequences of marital breakdown.

Conservative minister **Tim Yeo**, before the story of his mistress and child were revealed in 1994

Married with a family and therefore understands the needs of families. He is a man of integrity who believes in traditional moral values, discipline, and effective law and order.

Election address by Conservative MP **David Ashby**, 1992. He later unsuccessfully sued the *Sunday Times* for suggesting that he was a closet homosexual.

Family.

One of the 'recreations' listed by **Rod Richards** in parliamentary
biographical directory. He resigned in 1996 after allegations of an extra-
marital affair

The day hasn't yet arrived when an MP can be unseated by a gossip
columnist.

Maureen Colquhoun MP, after being outed as a lesbian by Nigel
Dempster in 1977. The day soon did. She lost her seat at the next election
in 1979

I see no reason why the mass of British business should find itself short
of money in the coming year ... Business is in a uniquely favourable
position today.

Denis Healey, Chancellor of the Exchequer, House of Commons, April
1974

There's a collapse of business confidence in Britain ...

Healey, September 1974

By the end of next year, we shall be on our way to that so-called economic miracle we need.

Healey, Budget broadcast, April 1976

If we can keep our heads – and our nerve – the long-awaited economic miracle is in our grasp.

Healey, July 1976

What I have always said is that no government can produce an economic miracle.

Healey, December 1976

Economic forecasts are no better than the long-range weather forecasts.
Healey, looking back on his chancellorship of 1974–79

Politically, the fall-out from the events of the last two weeks will be immense. There will be few politicians standing for election next time on a platform advocating 'free markets'.
Tony Blair, then Labour front-bench spokesman on economic affairs, on the stock market crash, October 1987

After the Budget, unemployment will rise this month, next month and for months afterwards.
Gordon Brown, shadow Chancellor, House of Commons, March 1993. It fell

There is no evidence at all of price increases stored up in the pipeline.
Shirley Williams, Prices and Consumer Protection Secretary, three days before polling day, October 1974. Inflation would continue to rise until it reached a record 26.9 per cent in the following August

The sacrifices called for will not be easy. This will be particularly the case in the early months of the policy because of price increases already in the pipeline.
Harold Wilson's anti-inflation White Paper, July 1975, introducing a £6 a week pay rise limit for all

To paraphrase Winston Churchill, I did not take the oath I have just taken with the intention of presiding over the dissolution of the world's strongest economy.

Ronald Reagan, inaugural presidential address, January 1981. Under his leadership, America's trade deficit multiplied six-fold, while the national debt tripled. The $2 *trillion* he added to the debt was more than all his predecessors combined

Sometimes I've heard it said that Conservatives have been associated with unemployment. That's absolutely wrong. We'd have been drummed out of office if we'd had this level of unemployment.

Margaret Thatcher, leader of the Opposition, party political broadcast, May 1977. Unemployment was then 1.3 million. It would exceed three million during her prime ministership, and would never be less than 1.3 million

I can say from my personal knowledge, without fear of contradiction, that he is a great benefactor of the wretched of the earth and ailing humanity in the present century.

Jam Sadiq, Pakistani provincial chief minister, defending the head of the BCCI bank, Agha Hasan Abedi, against speculation of fraud following the collapse of the bank in July 1991. Two months later, thirty-five senior executives at BCCI's headquarters in Abu Dhabi were arrested for fraud

Don't let the buggers get you down.

Conservative minister **Michael Mates**' inscription on a watch he gave to businessman and close friend Asil Nadir. Nadir was later arrested in Britain on fraud charges, jumped bail and fled to Cyprus in May 1993. Revelations about Mates' attempts to intervene on his behalf forced his resignation the following month

Nobody need be worried about BSE in this country or anywhere else.

John Gummer, Agriculture Minister, House of Commons, 1990

There is continued downturn in incidence of BSE.

Angela Browning, junior agriculture Minister, House of Commons, May 1995. By May 1996, BSE had affected 160,000 cattle on more than 30,000 farms

Beef is perfectly safe and a good product.

Douglas Hogg, Agriculture Minister, House of Commons, November 1995

Our policy has been one of total transparency. There is no way we can conceal evidence even if we wanted to.

Sir Kenneth Calman, Government Chief Medical Officer, December 1995

Even if science was wrong on that subject, we've removed from the human food chain the organs that could conceivably be linked to a transmission.

Stephen Dorrell, Health Secretary, December 1995

I would like to make a statement about the latest advice which the government has received from the Spongiform Encephalopathy Advisory Committee ... [it] has identified a previously unrecognized and consistent disease pattern ... the Committee have concluded that the most likely explanation at present is that these cases are linked to exposure to BSE.

Dorrell, House of Commons, May 1996

There is no need ... to revise ... advice on the safety of milk.

Dorrell, House of Commons, same day

The government has always assumed that maternal transmission [via milk] was theoretically possible.

Ministry of Agriculture press release, August 1996

The cumulative effects of the economic and financial sanctions might well bring the rebellion to an end within a matter of weeks rather than months.

Harold Wilson on Rhodesia crisis, January 1966, two months after the unilateral declaration of independence. (It took another fourteen years.)

I give Castro a year. No longer.

Fulgencio Batista, ousted Cuban dictator, 1959

The regime will not last long. It is in a period of terrible decadence. It is not a question of days, but perhaps a year, not more than that.

Romel Iglesias Gonzalez, head of Cuba's government-run radio, defecting to the United States, March 1991

Stick a fork in him, he's done.

James Baker, former US Secretary of State, predicting the imminent collapse of Fidel Castro's regime in Cuba after Castro had announced plans for economic reforms, March 1994

Russians for years have been changing their economy and approaching the abandonment of Communism, and the whole western world will be gratified at the happy climax of their efforts.

Tom Connally, senator from Texas and member of the Senate Foreign Relations Committee (and soon to be its chairman), analysing the significance of Stalin's disbandment of the Comintern, May 1943

I believe he [Stalin] is truly representative of the heart and soul of Russia; and I believe that we are going to get along very well with him and the Russian people.

Franklin Roosevelt, Christmas fireside chat radio broadcast 1943, after the Big Power war-time conferences at Teheran and Cairo

[Stalin has] something else in him besides this revolutionist Bolshevist thing ... I think that something [has] entered into his nature of the way in which a Christian gentleman should behave.

Roosevelt to his Cabinet, on his return from the Yalta conference, 1945.
He ascribed the special quality as having come from Stalin's early education for the priesthood.

Every year humanity takes a step towards Communism. Maybe not you, but at all events your grandson will surely be a Communist.

Nikita Khrushchev, to Sir William Hayter, British ambassador to Moscow, June 1956

Whether you like it or not, history is on our side. We will bury you.

Khrushchev, to western diplomats, Moscow, November 1956

We occupy second place in the world. We have left England behind ... We have also left France behind, and comrades, there is only America left. She can be compared to a worn-out runner. United States scientists have reported that Russia will overtake America in 1970. They are quite right. That is our date.

Khrushchev, 1959

The Communist Party has no God-given right to rule.

Mikhail Gorbachev, 1989

Workers of the world – we apologize.

Banner carried by reformist protestors in Moscow during a parade to commemorate the seventy-second anniversary of the Bolshevik revolution, 1989

It would have been better if the experiment had been conducted in some small country to make it clear that it was a Utopian idea.

Boris Yeltsin, on Communism, September 1991

The life of human beings is very short. We are all going to die. Why should we cling so much to power?

Muhammad Boudief, Algerian President, seconds before being assassinated, June 1992

The American disputes are settled and there is nothing to interrupt the peace and prosperity of the nation.

Lord North, Prime Minister, after removing all taxes (except on tea) imposed on the American colonies, April 1771

[There is] the fairest prospect of the continuance of peace that I have known in my lifetime.

Lord North, presenting his budget, May 1772. (The American War of Independence was less than three years away.)

Four or five frigates will do the business without any military force.

Lord North, on dealing with the rebellious American colonies, two years before the outbreak of war, House of Commons, 1774

So very contemptible is the rebel force now in all parts, and so vast is our superiority everywhere, that no resistance on their [the Americans'] part is to be apprehended that can materially obstruct the progress of the King's army in the speedy suppression of the rebellion.

Lord George Germain, Secretary of State for the colonies, 1781

The President's silly remarks.

US newspaper (unidentified) on Lincoln's Gettysburg Address, 1863, seen by one modern historian as 'the best short speech since the Sermon on the Mount'

Anything more dull and commonplace it wouldn't be easy to reproduce.

The Times (London), on the Address, 1863

He is not known except as a slang-whanging stump speaker of which all parties are ashamed.

Albany *Atlas and Argus*, on Abraham Lincoln's selection as Republican candidate, 1860 election

The conduct of the Republican Party in this nomination is a remarkable indication of the small intellect, growing smaller ... they take up a fourth-rate lecturer, who cannot speak good grammar, and who ... delivers hackneyed, illiterate compositions.

New York Herald

A horrid-looking wretch he is, sooty and scoundrelly in aspect, a cross between the nutmeg dealer, the horse swapper, and the night man, a creature fit evidently for petty treason, small stratagems and all sorts of spoils.

Charleston Mercury

Lincoln is the leanest, lankest, most ungainly mass of legs and arms and hatchet face ever strung on a single frame. He has most unwarrantably abused the privilege, which all politicians have, of being ugly.

Houston Telegraph

Tell us he resembles Jackson,
Save he wears a larger boot,
And is broader 'cross the shoulders,
And is taller by a foot.

Any lie we'll swallow -
Swallow any kind of mixture;
But O don't, we beg and pray you -
Don't for land's sake, show his picture.

Democratic Party campaign ballad, 1860 election.

It's a kangaroo ticket – stronger in the hindquarters than in the front.

Texan Democrat on the relative merits of the party's nomination of New York Governor Franklin Roosevelt for President and the more experienced congressman, John Garner, Speaker of the House, 1932

Here was a great convention ... nominating the weakest candidate before it.

H L Mencken, editor, the *American Mercury* of Roosevelt's nomination

... an amiable boy scout.

Walter Lippmann, celebrated American political commentator, on Roosevelt

The grass will grow in the streets of 100 cities.

Herbert Hoover, incumbent President, on prospects if his opponent Franklin Roosevelt won the election, campaign, 1932

They can beat him [Roosevelt] with a Chinaman.

H L Mencken, doyen of American political commentators, predicting the outcome of the 1936 election – which Roosevelt won by what still remains the largest ever margin of electoral college votes, 523 – 8

The main question is whether Governor Dewey will win by a fair margin or by a landslide.

New York Sun, a month before polling, October 1948

President Truman appears to be the only American who doesn't think Thomas E Dewey is going to be elected barring a political earthquake.

New York Daily News, two weeks before polling, October 1948

It is a godsend to this country and to the world at large that Harry Truman will get his dismissal notice next Tuesday.

San Francisco Chronicle, a week before polling, October 1948

Truman put up a courageous fight, but ... he cannot possibly win.

Baltimore Sun, eve of polling, November 1948

'DEWEY DEFEATS TRUMAN'

Chicago Daily Tribune headline, day after polling, still getting it wrong on the outcome of the 1948 presidential election

We have the happiest Africans in the world.

Ian Smith, Rhodesian Prime Minister, November 1971

There are going to be no dramatic changes in Rhodesia.

Smith, January 1975

I don't believe in black majority rule in Rhodesia ... not in a thousand years.

Smith, March 1976

We live in a world of rapid change, and if we are to survive in such a world we must be prepared to subject ourselves to change.

Smith, September 1976

If I have anything to do with it, any handover of power to the Patriotic Front will not take place.

Smith, July 1977

I have got to admit that things haven't gone quite the way I wanted.

Smith, June 1979

If we find Ian Smith alive when we take power, he will be tried by a People's Court and, I hope, shot.

Robert Mugabe, Patriotic Front leader, March 1978

I have met with Mr Smith and we agreed to co-operate.
Mugabe, March 1980

Mugabe is a Marxist terrorist ... an Apostle of Satan.
Ian Smith, before Mugabe's takeover in Rhodesia/Zimbabwe

He's sober and responsible. He's a pragmatist.
and his government will probably be the best in Africa.
Smith, after Mugabe's takeover

If Germany is to become a colonizing power, all I say is 'God speed her.' She becomes our ally and partner in the execution of the great purposes of Providence for the advantage of mankind.
William Gladstone, Prime Minister, 1885

We can now look forward with something like confidence to the time when war between civilized nations will be considered as antiquated as a duel.
George Peabody Gooch MP, 1906–10, shortly after losing his seat in the House of Commons, in *History of Our Time* (1911)

Happily there seems to be no reason why we should be anything but spectators [of the approaching war].
Herbert Asquith, Prime Minister, July 1914

It is the greatest step towards Socialism that could possibly have been made. We shall have Labour governments in every country after this.

Sir Edward Grey, Foreign Secretary, August 1914, on the probable consequences of the First World War

You will be home before the leaves have fallen from the trees.

Kaiser Wilhelm II of Germany, addressing troops leaving for the Western Front, August 1914

What is our task? To make Britain a fit country for heroes to live in.

Lloyd George, Prime Minister, shortly after the Armistice ending the First World War, 1918

The League of Nations grows in moral courage. Its frown will soon be more dreaded than a nation's arms, and when that happens you and I shall have security and peace.

Ramsay MacDonald, Prime Minister, on the ill-fated League which proved toothless and powerless in the 1930s. Lord Mayor's banquet speech, November 1929

For what? A war with Japan! But why should there be a war with Japan? I do not believe there is the slightest chance of it in our lifetime.

Winston Churchill, Chancellor of the Exchequer, to Prime Minister Stanley Baldwin, opposing the Admiralty's plans for rearming the navy, December 1924

When I agreed in principle to the base at Singapore, I had never imagined that that decision would be used as a peg on which to hang far-reaching schemes of alarmist policy and consequential armament. I do not believe there is any danger to be apprehended from Japan.

Churchill, reiterating his opposition to British naval strengthening in the Far East, Committee of Imperial Defence, July 1926

I am going to say something to you which is very unfashionable – a word of sympathy for Japan. I do not think the League of Nations would be well advised to have a quarrel with Japan.

Churchill, on Japan's conquest of Manchuria, House of Commons, February 1933

So great a man ... so wise a ruler.

Churchill on Mussolini, September 1935

If I had been an Italian, I should have been on Mussolini's side fifteen years ago.

Churchill, July 1937

If I may judge from my personal knowledge of Herr Hitler, peace and justice are the key-words of his policy.

Sir Thomas Moore MP, October 1933

[My visits to Germany] have given me the impression that there is almost no Great Power with which we are less likely to become involved in war than Germany.

Moore, in *The Times*, May 1935

Far too many people have an erroneous conception of what the National Socialist regime really stands for. Otherwise they would lay less stress on Nazi dictatorship and much more emphasis on the great social experiment which is being tried out.

Sir Nevile Henderson, British ambassador to Germany, June 1937

Those who imagine that Germany has swung back to its old imperial temper cannot have any understanding of the character of the change. The idea of a Germany intimidating Europe with a threat that its irresistible army might march across frontiers forms no part in the new vision ... they have no longer the desire themselves to invade any other land.

Lloyd George, former Prime Minister, writing on his return from visiting Hitler's Germany, *Daily Express*, September 1936

I shall never forget the extraordinarily interesting tour which you organized for me and my friends in Germany last year, during which I had the privilege of meeting the great leader of a great people. I have never doubted the fundamental greatness of Herr Hitler as a man even in moments of profound disagreement with his policy ... I have never withdrawn one particle of the admiration which I personally felt for him and expressed on my return from Germany.

Lloyd George, on his meeting with Hitler in September 1936, letter to friend, December 1937

The worst thing Neville Chamberlain ever did was to meet Hitler and let Hitler see him.

Lloyd George, on the outbreak of war, September 1939

We cannot tell whether Hitler will be the man who will once again let loose upon the world another war ... or whether he will go down in history as the man who restored honour and peace of mind to the great Germanic nation and brought it back serene, helpful and strong, to the forefront of the European family circle.

Winston Churchill, 1935

Germany has been transformed since my last visit several years ago ... the Reich is the miracle of the twentieth century.

William Knudsen, president of General Motors, October 1938

I do not think there is the slightest prospect of any war. I know ... how rash it is to prophesy as to the future of international affairs. But never-theless I do not believe that there is anyone in this room who will con-tradict me when I say that there has scarcely ever been a period in the world's history when war seemed less likely than it does at present.

Viscount Cecil, the British government representative, opening the League of Nations Assembly session in Geneva, September 1931. A week later Japan invaded Manchuria, the first major challenge for the League. Its failure to settle the dispute started the downward spiral to the Second World War

Herr Hitler is no longer a problem; his movement has ceased to be a political danger and the whole problem is solved. It is a thing of the past.

General Kurt von Schleicher, Chancellor of Germany, 15 January 1933. He had become Chancellor six weeks earlier; his government fell a fortnight later when Hitler took over

No danger at all. We've hired him for our act.

Franz von Papen, Chancellor of Germany June–December 1932 and new Vice-Chancellor, on Hitler's appointment as Chancellor at the head of a coalition Cabinet limited to containing just two other Nazis, January 1933

It is [Hitler's] set purpose … to re-establish Germany on a footing of equality with other nations; and the internal excesses of his regime should not debar foreign statesmanship from examining with an open mind the external claims of the German … government.

The Times, on the new Hitler government, March 1933

War will not come again … [Germany has] a more profound impression than any other of the evil that war causes; Germany's problems cannot be settled by war.

Adolf Hitler, interview in *Daily Mail*, August 1934

I give you my word that there will be no great armaments.

Stanley Baldwin, Prime Minister, speech to the International Peace Society, general election campaign, October 1935

The League of Nations will remain … the keystone of British foreign policy. … We shall take no action in isolation, but we shall be prepared to take our part in any collective action decided upon by the League …

National Government election manifesto, November 1935 (before the Anglo–Italian agreement in 1937, the four-power Czech settlement in 1938, the 1939 unilateral British guarantee of Poland and the Anglo-French negotiations with Russia in the same year).

Herr Hitler made a statement ... holding out the olive branch ... which ought to be taken at face value. ... It is idle to say these statements are insincere.

Arthur Greenwood, Labour deputy leader, on Hitler's march into the Rhineland and his simultaneous statement that 'Germany has no further territorial claims of any sort in Europe', House of Commons, March 1936

After all, they are only going into their own back garden.

Lord Lothian, on Hitler's remilitarization of the Rhineland, March 1936

There is today a good prospect of restoring those old friendly relations [with Italy] which, until they were recently broken [over the invasion of Abyssinia], have lasted so long that they had become almost traditional between our two countries. ... I only ask you to have a little patience ... before our agreement with Italy is concluded and published, and then if you are not of my opinion, if you do not believe that it is not the Prime Minister who has been fooled ... I will be prepared to eat my hat.

Neville Chamberlain, speaking on appeasement plans with Mussolini's Italy, April 1938

I frankly confess my deep disappointment at an action by the Italian government which has cast a shadow over the genuineness of their intentions to carry out their undertakings.

Chamberlain, preparing to eat his hat twelve months later, after Mussolini's invasion of Albania, April 1939

Czechoslovakia is not of the remotest concern to us.

Daily Mail article by owner Lord Rothermere, May 1938

Britain never gave any pledge to protect Czechoslovakia. ... No moral obligation rests upon us.

Daily Express, statements by *its* owner Lord Beaverbrook, 22 September 1938 (on the morning of Chamberlain's second visit to Hitler)

In spite of the hardness and ruthlessness I thought I saw in his face, I got the impression that here was a man who could be relied upon when he had given his word.

Neville Chamberlain, writing to his sister, after his first meeting with Hitler, Berchtesgaden, September 1938

A quarrel in a far-away country between people of whom we know nothing.

Chamberlain, characterizing the crisis between Germany and Czechoslovakia over the Sudetenland, September 1938

[Hitler] would not deliberately deceive a man whom he respected and with whom he had been in negotiation.

Chamberlain reporting to Cabinet, after second meeting with Hitler, Bad Godesberg, September 1938

However much we may sympathize with a small nation confronted by a big and powerful neighbour, we cannot in all circumstances undertake to involve the whole British Empire in a war simply on her account.

Chamberlain, during Czech crisis, September 1938. A maxim in vogue in the Foreign Office while Chamberlain made his three visits to Hitler during the crisis ran:

If at first you don't concede
Fly, fly, fly again.

Peace with honour ... I believe it is peace for our time.

Chamberlain, speaking to the crowd in Downing Street, on the Munich Agreement, September 1938

No conqueror returning from a victory on the battlefield has come home adorned with nobler laurels than Mr Chamberlain from Munich yesterday. ... There have been times when such a manifesto [the joint Anglo–German declaration of peace] could be dismissed as a pious platitude. ... The present, it is fair to think, is not such a time.

The Times leader, 'A New Dawn', on the morning after Chamberlain's return from Munich, October 1938

It is my hope, and my belief, that under the new system of guarantees, the new Czechoslovakia will find a greater security than she has ever enjoyed in the past.

Neville Chamberlain, House of Commons, October 1938

I myself believe that the international guarantee in which we have taken part will more than compensate for the loss of the strategic frontier.

Sir Samuel Hoare, Home Secretary, and former Foreign Secretary, defending the Munich settlement, October 1938. Hitler would invade five months later.

We never guaranteed the frontiers as they existed. What we did was to guarantee against unprovoked aggression – quite a different thing.

Neville Chamberlain, House of Commons, November 1938, equivocating after Hitler and Mussolini made border alterations in Czechoslovakia to Hungary's favour without consulting Britain, just a month after Munich

There will be no great war in Europe in 1939.

Daily Express, 2 January 1939

No man that I know is less tempted than Mr Chamberlain to cherish unreal illusions.

Lord Halifax, Foreign Secretary, February 1939

For the Polish Corridor, no British government ever will or ever can risk the bones of a British grenadier.

Austen Chamberlain, half brother of Neville, Foreign Secretary, February 1925

In the event of any action which clearly threatened Polish independence and which the Polish government accordingly considered it vital
to resist ... Her Majesty's Government would feel themselves bound at
once to lend the Polish government all support in their power. They
have given the Polish government an assurance to this effect.

Neville Chamberlain, announcing the Polish guarantee, House of
Commons, March 1939

War today is not only not inevitable, but it is unlikely.

Sir Thomas Inskip, Minister for Co-ordination of Defence, August 1939

No enemy bomber can reach the Ruhr. If one reaches the Ruhr, my
name is not Goering. You can call me Meyer.

Hermann Goering, Nazi air force minister, addressing the Luftwaffe, 1939

The Americans cannot build aeroplanes. They are very good at refriger-
ators and razor blades.

Goering, assuring Hitler of the unlikelihood of American air raids on
Germany, 1940

I'm an experienced fighter pilot myself. I know what is possible. But I
know what isn't too ... I officially assert that American fighter planes
did not reach Aachen. ... I herewith give you an official order that they
weren't there.

Goering, on being told that an Allied fighter had been shot down over
German territory, disproving the official view that the Allies did not have a
long-range fighter escort capacity, 1943

It has been assumed, in my opinion erroneously, that Japan covets these islands [the Philippines]. Just why has never been satisfactorily explained. Proponents of such a theory fail fully to credit the logic of the Japanese mind.

General Douglas MacArthur, 1939. Japan invaded the Philippines three days after Pearl Harbor in 1941

If Japan chose war, the tremendous odds against her would limit the hostilities to a relatively brief period. Should the conflict last six months, a not unreasonably optimistic estimate, the spring of 1942 would see the release of large military and naval forces for action in Europe and the Atlantic.

New Republic, a month before Pearl Harbor, 1941

Japan will be overcome within six months. Her military strength has been sapped by her operations in China. Her economic conditions have been more and more seriously strained ... Authorities credit her with a good navy but surely the combined fleets of America and Britain should speedily overmatch it.

Forbes Magazine, December 1941, shortly after Pearl Harbor

Defeat of Germany means defeat of Japan, probably without firing a shot.

President Roosevelt, supporting the 'Europe first' war strategy, July 1942

The British are such clever propagandists, they might well have cooked up the story.

US Congresswoman **Jeanette Rankin**, casting the only negative vote against the declaration of war on Japan the day after Pearl Harbor, December 1941

Hitler's missed the bus.

Neville Chamberlain, House of Commons, 4 April 1940, after the winter of inaction dubbed the 'phoney war' and the 'bore war' which had allowed British forces to build up in France, leading Chamberlain to see a negotiated peace as the most likely outcome. Five days later, Hitler invaded Denmark and Norway; and in May, Holland, Belgium and France

The entry of the United States into the war is of no consequence at all for Germany ... The United States will not be a threat to us for decades – not in 1945 but at the earliest in 1970 or 1980.

Adolf Hitler, responding to Soviet Foreign Minister Molotov's concerns about reports of US assistance to Britain, summit meeting, 12 November 1940 (at which time Hitler and Stalin were still technically allies).

We will stay friends with you, whatever happens.

Joseph Stalin, to Hans Krebs, acting German military attaché at public diplomatic gathering, Moscow, April 1941. The two dictatorships had signed a non-aggression pact in August 1939. Hitler would invade Russia two months later

Nobody now fears that a Japanese fleet could deal an unexpected blow on our Pacific possessions ... Radio makes surprise impossible.

Josephus Daniels, former US Secretary of the Navy, 1922

Russia is likely to come out of the war the greatest democracy in the world.

Capt. Eddie Rickenbacker, special representative of President Roosevelt, after visit to Russia, 1943

There will no longer be need for spheres of influence, for alliances ... or any other of the special arrangements through which ... nations strove to safeguard their security or to promote their interests.

Cordell Hull, US Secretary of State, on his vision of the post-war world, address to Congress, November 1943

Never in the past has there been any place on the globe where the vital interests of American and Russian people have clashed or even been antagonistic, and there is no reason to suppose there should be now or in the future ever such a place.

Dean Acheson, US Under-Secretary of State, 1945

[The Yalta Conference] spells the end of the system of unilateral action, the exclusive alliances, the spheres of influence, the balances of power, and all the other expedients that have been tried for centuries – and have always failed.

President Roosevelt, addressing Congress after the Big Three conference with Stalin and Churchill on the post-war settlement, March 1945

[NATO is] a stop-gap and a stop-gap only.

Philip Noel-Baker, Foreign Office minister, introducing the North Atlantic Treaty Organization treaty to the House of Commons for approval, May 1949. NATO continues to this day, nearly fifty years on.

Our defensive perimeter runs from the Aleutians [off Alaska] to Japan, the Ryukyus [Okinawa] and down to the Philippines ... So far as the military security of other areas in the Pacific is concerned, it must be clear that no person can guarantee these areas against military attack. But it must also be clear that such a guarantee is hardly ... necessary ...

Dean Acheson, US Secretary of State, speech to the National Press Club, January 1950. His perimeter excluded Korea, and all American forces had just been withdrawn from the peninsula the previous year. The omission is widely believed to have encouraged the North to invade the South, which they did five months later

Very little. Had they interfered in the first or second months, it would have been decisive. We are no longer fearful of their intervention.

General Douglas MacArthur, commander of allied forces in Korea, September 1950, responding to President Truman's enquiry about the chances of Chinese intervention in the war. Two months later, 850,000 Chinese invaded

[Nasser] is the best sort of Egyptian and a great improvement on the Pashas of the past.

Anthony Eden, then Foreign Secretary, to the Conservative 1922 Committee, after meeting Nasser in Cairo, February 1955

I was asked ... whether our sovereignty was jeopardized and I am saying frankly that it is not.

Alexander Dubček, leader of the Prague Spring reforms in Czechoslovakia, press conference, August 1968, days before the Soviet invasion

The major part of the US military task [in Vietnam] can be completed by the end of 1965.

Robert McNamara, US Defense Secretary, after visit to South Vietnam, October 1962.

Our diplomatic reports indicate that the opposing forces no longer really expect a military victory in South Vietnam.

President Lyndon Johnson, 1966

Our staying power is what counts in the long and dangerous months ahead. The Communists expect us to lose heart ... they believe political disagreements in Washington, and confusion and doubt in the United States, will hand them victory in South Vietnam. They are wrong.

Johnson, 1967

I seriously doubt if we will have another war. This [Vietnam] is probably the last.

President Richard Nixon, 1973

The honeymoon period [is] coming to an end, but it has not ended in divorce or a stand-up fight between husband and wife. The troops have been accepted by both communities and a happy, comfortable married life [is] under way.

Denis Healey, Defence Secretary, visiting Northern Ireland a month after the introduction of British troops to control sectarian troubles, September 1969

Our judgement is that the presence of the Royal Marines garrison ... is sufficient deterrent against any possible aggression.

Margaret Thatcher, February 1982, six weeks before the Argentinian invasion of the Falklands

The British won't fight.

Leopoldo Galtieri, President of Argentina, to US Secretary of State Alexander Haig a week after the Argentine invasion of the Falklands, April 1982

The task force involves enormous risks. I say that it will cost this country a far greater humiliation than we have already suffered ... The attempt will fail.

Tony Benn, April 1982, on plans to recapture the Falklands

Iran is an island of stability in one of the most volatile parts of the world.

President Jimmy Carter, 1977

It is unlikely that Iran could go to war in the next five to ten years with its current inventory without US support on a day-to-day basis.

US Senate Foreign Relations Committee report, 1977, before the overthrow of the Shah. The Iran–Iraq war broke out in 1980 and lasted until 1988, the longest conventional war of the twentieth century

Let us demonstrate to the world, as generations of Americans have done before us, that when Americans take on a challenge, they do the job right.

President-elect **Bill Clinton**, on the 'invasion' of Somalia by US marines to restore peace in Somalia in Operation Restore Hope, December 1992. Most of the troops were withdrawn by the following May and the task handed over to the United Nations. The rest left in March 1994, and the general view was that the mission had been a failure

This is not war. This is not Vietnam. It is not Somalia. It is not Lebanon.

Richard Holbrooke, US Assistant Secretary of State, minimizing the risks involved in sending 20,000 American troops to Bosnia, December 1995

5 *Well ...*

On Second Thoughts ...

We may be surprised, not only by events but by revisions
to our own attitudes. Opinions change. The record
endures. Those whose job it is to regale the public with
pronouncements face, in a long career, an unenviable
choice: shall they repeat themselves or contradict
themselves? Here are a few who chose the latter ...

I never should be so presumptuous as to think myself capable of
directing the departments of others ... I do not think our constitution
authorizes such a character as that animal called a Prime Minister.

Lord North, Prime Minister, House of Commons, May 1778

[Affairs of state] can hardly be well conducted unless there is a person
in the Cabinet capable of leading, of discerning between opinions, of
deciding quickly and confidently, and connecting all the operations of
government ...

Lord North to King George III, summer 1778

Conservatism discards Prescription, shrinks from Principle, disavows Progress; ... it offers no redress for the present and makes no preparation for the future.

Benjamin Disraeli, future Conservative Prime Minister, *Coningsby*, 1844

These wretched colonies ... are a millstone round our necks.

Bejamin Disraeli, Chancellor of the Exchequer, 1852

In my opinion no minister in this country will do his duty who neglects any opportunity of reconstructing as much as possible our colonial empire, and of responding to those distant sympathies which may become the source of incalculable strength and happiness to this land.

Disraeli, Opposition leader, 1872

One of the greatest of Romans, when asked what were his policies, replied, *Imperium et Libertas* [Empire and Liberty]. That would not make a bad programme for a British ministry.

Disraeli, Prime Minister, Mansion House speech, 1879

In politics, there is no use looking beyond the next fortnight.

Joseph Chamberlain, President of the Local Government Board under Gladstone and future Colonial Secretary, 1886

It is said that the City is the centre of the world's finance, that the fate of our manufactures therefore is a secondary consideration; ... Now, I ask you, gentlemen, whether ... that is not a very short-sighted view.

Chamberlain, speech to City financiers, London Guildhall, 1904

We must not attach too much importance to these frothings of Sir Edward Carson. I daresay when the worst comes to the worst, we shall find that civil war evaporates in uncivil words.

Winston Churchill, then Home Secretary, dismissing the threat from
Ulster Unionists led by Carson of violent resistance to Irish Home Rule,
October 1911

Much is to be apprehended from a combination of the rancour of a party in the ascendant and the fanaticism of these stubborn and determined Orangemen.

Churchill, changing his mind, August 1913

There is no need to assume the use of force, or, indeed, to talk about it. Such talk is to be strongly deprecated. Not only can it do no good; it is bound to do harm. It must interfere with the progress of diplomacy, and it must increase feelings of insecurity and uncertainty.

Neville Chamberlain, House of Commons, opposing calls to warn
Germany not to use force, beginning of the Sudetenland crisis, March 1938

Our past experience has shown us only too clearly that weakness in armed strength means weakness in diplomacy, and if we want to secure a lasting peace ... diplomacy cannot be effective unless the consciousness exists ... that behind the diplomacy is the strength to give effect to it.

Chamberlain, House of Commons, debate on the Munich Agreement
which – temporarily – bought off Hitler at the expense of Czechoslovakia,
October 1938

I myself have always deprecated ... in crisis after crisis, appeals to the Dunkirk spirit as an answer to our problems.

Harold Wilson, on Harold Macmillan's use of the patriotic tag during
economic difficulties, 1961

I believe that the spirit of Dunkirk will once again carry us through to success.

Wilson, now Prime Minister, on his own government's handling of economic difficulties, speech to the party conference, 1964

What the Tories propose [entry into the EEC at the first favourable opportunity] would mean an unacceptable increase in the cost of living ... an unacceptable increase in our imports bill ... and a total disruption of our trade with Commonwealth countries.

Wilson, during general election campaign, March 1966

Our purpose is to make a reality of the unity of Western Europe. ... This indeed is something that we have striven for for many years, and I am convinced that if Britain is a member of a united European Community, the chances of our achieving this will be immeasurably greater.

Wilson, Prime Minister, House of Commons, May 1967

I can really see significant long-term opportunities for ordinary people in Britain and in the Six if we could persuade the British public to vote for entry.

Tony Benn, Bristol speech, July 1971

Britain's continuing membership of the Community would mean the end of Britain as a completely self-governing nation.

Benn, letter to constituents, December 1974

I want to put Britain at the very heart of Europe.

John Major, Bonn summit, 1991

We don't want a negative, tentative Britain.
Major, 7 April 1992

I am the biggest Euro-sceptic in the Cabinet.
Major, soon afterwards

The rule of law should be upheld by all political parties. They should neither advise others to break the law, nor encourage others to do so even when they strongly disagree with the legislation put forward by the Government of the day.
James Callaghan, Labour shadow employment spokesman, 1972

If the law is a bad law, there is always the contingent right to take action that you would not otherwise take.
Callaghan, retired leader of the Labour Party, 1982

May I remind the House that many of the most progressive and far-reaching educational changes were made by Conservative education ministers ... among those changes which took place ... was the movement in Conservative counties towards a new comprehensive system.
Margaret Thatcher, first speech as Education Secretary, July 1970. In her first three years in office, she received nearly 2,700 proposals for schemes of comprehensive education, and rejected only 115, or less than 4 per cent of them. She approved more comprehensive schools and closed more grammar schools than any other education secretary.

The next Conservative government will look forward to discussion and consultation with the trade union movement about the policies that are now needed to save our country.

Thatcher, speech to party conference, Brighton, October 1976

The enemy within.

Thatcher's reported view of trade unions, during miners' strike, 1984

Where there is discord, may we bring harmony;
Where there is error, may we bring truth;
Where there is doubt, may we bring faith;
Where there is despair, may we bring hope.

Thatcher, quoting lines attributed to St Francis of Assisi, outside 10 Downing Street, on taking office as Prime Minister, May 1979

We are not in politics to ignore people's worries; we are in politics to deal with them.

Thatcher

Many of our troubles are due to the fact that our people turn to politicians for everything.

Thatcher

We must build a society in which each citizen can develop his full potential, both for his own benefit and for the community as a whole.

Thatcher, 1975

We must learn again to be one nation or one day we shall be no nation.

Thatcher, 1978

The mission of this government is much more than the promotion of economic progress. It is to renew the spirit and solidarity of the nation.
Thatcher, July 1979

There is no such thing as Society. There are individual men and women, and there are families.
Thatcher, 1987

Civil servants have not got the expertise at their disposal which a merchant bank has. If they had such expertise, they would probably be working very successfully for a merchant bank.
Thatcher, House of Commons, 1967

The sheer professionalism of the British civil service, which allows governments to come and go with a minimum of dislocation and a maximum of efficiency, is something other countries with different systems have every cause to envy.
Thatcher, memoirs, 1993

They have hit at everything I believed in.
Thatcher on her successor John Major's government, 12 June 1995

I don't think I was unkind to him. I supported him a lot – I chose him!
Thatcher, 23 June 1995

Get Cracking!
Thatcher, 9 October 1996, urging Conservatives to work for Major.

You turn if you want to. The lady's not for turning.
Thatcher, party conference 1980

We secured stable exchange rates in the ERM – and we'll keep our position there.

John Major, election rally, April 1992

The Exchange Rate Mechanism is not an optional extra, an add-on to be jettisoned at the first hint of trouble. It has been and will remain at the heart of our macro-economic policy.

Norman Lamont, Chancellor, July 1992

I was under no illusions when I took Britain into the ERM. I said at the time that membership was no soft option. The soft option, the devaluer's option, the inflationary option, would be a betrayal of our future ... there is going to be no devaluation, no realignment.

John Major, speech to the Scottish Confederation of British Industry conference, 10 September 1992. Six days later, on 'Black Wednesday', Britain withdrew from the ERM

It is clear that we must not go back into the ERM.

Norman Lamont, addressing the Conservative Party conference, October 1992

It is inconceivable that we could transform this society without a major extension of public ownership.

Neil Kinnock, *Marxism Today*, 1983

The kind of economy we are faced with is going to be a market economy and we have got to make it work better than the Tories.

Kinnock, Labour Party conference, 1988

There is nothing in the Labour Party constitution that could or should prevent people from holding opinions which favour Leninist-Trotskyism.

Kinnock, then shadow education spokesman, *Broad Left Alliance* journal, October 1982

Maggot extremists.

Kinnock, Labour leader, describing Militant Tendency activists, February 1986

The mild tinkering with the economy proposed by the Social Democrats nowhere near measures up to the problem. A massive reconstruction of industry is needed ... the resources required to reconstruct manufacturing industry call for enormous state guidance and intervention.

Tony Blair, before his election as an MP, 1982

Without an active, interventionist industrial policy ... Britain faces the future of having to compete on dangerously unequal terms in the EC.

Blair, shadow industry spokesman, May 1988

New Labour does not believe it is the job of government to interfere in the running of business.

Blair, speech to Nottingham Chamber of Commerce, January 1996

The extraordinary proposition [is] advanced that it is the proper role of the government to interfere in the due process of a voluntary organization ... It is thoroughly unconscionable and wrong to tell trade unions how to run elections.

Blair, backbencher, opposing the Trade Union Bill requiring unions to hold secret ballots before strike action, House of Commons, November 1983

Having fought long and hard for [their freedoms, unions] will not give them up lightly. We shall oppose the Bill which is a scandalous and undemocratic measure against the trade union movement.

Blair, on the same Bill, 1983

The basic elements of that legislation: ballots before strikes, for union elections [and] restrictions on mass picketing are here to stay.

Blair, Labour leader, November 1994

Heavens above, that is common sense.

Blair, asked whether he would keep the trade union legislation of the 1980s, April 1995

There is no going back on the Thatcherite trade union reforms.

Blair, quoted *Daily Telegraph*, January 1996

Parliamentary Labour CND supports the removal of all nuclear weapons from British territory and expresses its solidarity with all campaigners for Peace.

Blair, Labour front-bench spokesman, advert signed by him in *Sanity*, May 1986

Labour will retain Britain's nuclear capability, with the number of warheads no greater than the present total.

Blair, still before he became party leader, April 1992

[British Airways] will be the pantomime horse of capitalism if it is anything at all.

Donald Dewar, Labour front-bench spokesman, on the privatization of British Airways, House of Commons, November 1979

Privatized utilities like Telecom and gas and essential industries such as British Airways and Rolls-Royce were sold off by the Tories in the closest thing, post-war, to legalized political corruption ... in fact it was a unique form of corruption since we were bribed with our own money.

Tony Blair, *News on Sunday*, November 1987

The great utilities must be treated as public services and should be owned by the public.

Blair, *Enterprise for Labour*, July 1989

Let me make it crystal clear that any privatization of the railway system which is there on the arrival of a Labour government will be quickly and effectively returned to public ownership.

John Prescott, Labour front-bench spokesman, September 1993

I am not about to start spraying around commitments as to what we are going to do when the government carries through its proposals.

Tony Blair, Labour leader, *Daily Telegraph*, January 1995

I am not going to get into a situation where I am declaring that the Labour government is going to commit sums of money to renationalization several years down the line.

Blair, January 1995

The EEC has pushed up prices, especially for food ... Above all, the EEC takes away Britain's freedom to follow the sort of economic policies we need. These are just two of the reasons for coming out.

Blair, campaigning in the Beaconsfield by-election, 1982

We'll negotiate a withdrawal from the EEC which has drained our natural resources and destroyed jobs.

Blair, election address, general election 1983

I have always believed that our country can prosper best within Europe.

Blair, June 1994

I always believed that it was important for Britain to be in Europe ...

Blair, Labour leader, December 1994

Leaving the European Union ... would not merely be disastrous for jobs and industry. It would relegate Britain from the premier division of nations with influence and standing.

'New Labour' manifesto, July 1996

Labour is committed to a regional assembly for Wales and to regional assemblies for England.

Tony Blair, during Labour leadership contest, June 1994

There is not a consensus about regional assemblies in England. ... We are not committed to regional assemblies in England.

Blair, Labour leader, March 1995

Yes, we are against a single currency.

John Prescott, Labour front-bench spokesman, June 1991

I am not a fan of a single currency, no.

Prescott, July 1994

Would the Prime Minister be in favour of persuading the country that it was right to join a single currency? I say yes to that.

Tony Blair, Labour leader, House of Commons, March 1995

The issue of the single currency must be determined by a hard-headed look at its economic practicalities. For Britain, we would need to be convinced that economic conditions would allow it to succeed. We will therefore reserve our options on it.

'New Labour' manifesto, July 1996

I don't actually favour putting a target on it.

Tony Blair, Labour leader, on full employment, BBC TV, 12 June 1994

I believe we will have to set ourselves a target ... I don't think the public are going to be satisfied with rhetoric.

John Prescott, Labour deputy leader, *Guardian*, 13 June 1994

Without ideas, there is no point in being in politics.

Jack Straw, Labour front-bench spokesman, *Oldham Chronicle*, October 1986

I am a working politician, not a thinker.

Straw, *The Times*, February 1989

Markets are poor means of securing welfare and neither the only nor the best way of allocating resources.

Straw, *Guardian*, September 1984

We must recognize that a nation of consumers enjoying relatively high living standards becomes literally much more choosy, much more interested in choice and variety. The aspirations of choice are now spreading from consumer goods to public services and rightly so.

Straw, *Guardian*, March 1988

We object to the private ownership of capital because of the unacceptable and undemocratic power over other people and over vast resources which it gives to those who hold such concentrations of wealth.

Straw, *Guardian*, September 1984

Karl Marx would have supported the policy of Labour's policy review ... for this process is genuinely dialectical. It is a great pity that Marx's alleged disciples today can't see that.

Straw, *Financial Times*, July 1988

The basic ideas of socialism – full employment, redistribution of wealth and power, equality, public ownership, collective provision – are as relevant in the 1990s as they were in 1945.

John Prescott, Labour front-bench spokesman, June 1988

I believe in Clause Four – I think there is a role for it.

Prescott, July 1994

Clause Four was never intended as anything other than something to inspire party activists ... no Labour government could ever implement anything like Clause Four.

Jack Straw, Labour Party press release, December 1994

Yes, it's the politics of envy. We're envious of their [company directors'] wealth. These people are stinking lousy thieving incompetent scum.

Frank Dobson, Labour frontbencher, The *Sun*, September 1992

We will ensure that the undeserving rich, the real beneficiaries of the something-for-nothing society, put something back into society.

Gordon Brown, Labour Party press release, September 1994

Britain needs successful people in business who can become rich by their success, through the money they earn.

Tony Blair, Labour leader, speech to Confederation of British Industry, 1995

There are some things we can do on our own. We can abandon the pretence of a British independent deterrent.

David Steel, Liberal party leader, 1982

We will maintain the deterrent capacity for as long as it is needed.

Steel, co-leader Liberal/SDP Alliance, general election camapaign, 1987

We are fed up with fudging and mudging.

David Owen, Labour Party conference, shortly before formation of the breakaway SDP, 1980.

What is needed is a *socialist* philosophy outside the restrictive confines of much of the present polarized political debate.

Owen, hardback edition of *Face the Future*, published 1981 (before he led the founding of the breakaway SDP)

What is needed is a *political* philosophy outside the restrictive confines of much of the present polarized political debate.

Owen, paperback edition of *Face the Future*, published later in 1981 (after the formation of the SDP) (our italics)

I feel a degree of regret that Marshall did not push on and say 'abolish the GLC' because I think it would have been a major saving and would have released massive resources for more productive use.

Ken Livingstone, 1979, then an Opposition Labour councillor, on the 1977 Marshall Report on the future of the Greater London Council. When later Leader of the GLC, he fought a high profile campaign against abolition legislation in the mid-1980s.

I am very glad to support the Energy Conservation Bill. It is long overdue. I shall urge the government to support it.

Robert Jones, then a backbench MP, 1993

I deplore the Bill ... Frankly, we have much more practical things to get on with.

Jones, now Minister for Energy Conservation, 1994

The Labour Party is committed to the reintroduction of public ownership of the coal industry.

Martin O'Neill, Opposition energy spokesman, House of Commons, March 1994

While we envisage a national role for coal in our energy strategy, we do not intend to re-nationalize the industry.

O'Neill, speech to the Coal Industry Society conference, November 1994

There has been no change in Labour's policy.

O'Neill, letter to *Guardian*, November 1994

Not only Celtic nationalists feel the need for a significant shift of power away from the centre of British politics ... One practical answer could be the creation of new regional parliaments. They could strengthen the working of democracy in their areas. With some devolution of powers, they could also take a lot of the workload off Parliament.

Kenneth Clarke, future Chancellor and opponent of devolution in the 1990s, Birmingham Bow Group pamphlet, 1968

To spend many years in prison for a crime you did not commit is both a terrible thing and one for which release from prison and financial recompense can make amends. Even this injustice cannot be compared to the icy comfort of a posthumous pardon. We cannot but be relieved that the death penalty was not available when we consider the irreparable damage which would have been inflicted on the criminal justice system in this country had innocent people been executed.

Michael Howard, Home Secretary, during Commons debate on restoring the death penalty, February 1994. He had previously campaigned for restoration, and voted in its favour in 1990. *'Howard: His league of penal reform is hang 'em'* ran the headline in *Today* when he became Home Secretary in 1993.

This is the run-up to the big match which, in my view, should be a walkover.

Rear-Admiral Sandy Woodward, commander of the Falklands task force, after the successful capture of South Georgia, 1982

[It] could prove a long and bloody campaign.

Woodward, forty-eight hours later.

We have stood apart, studiously neutral.

President Woodrow Wilson, speech to Congress, December 1915, about the Great War

America cannot be an ostrich with its head in the sand.
Wilson, speech in Des Moines two months later, February 1916

Government, after all, is a very simple thing.
Warren Harding, US President 1921–3, campaign trail

I can't make a damn thing out of this tax problem. I listen to one side and they seem right – and then I talk to the other side and they seem just as right, and here I am where I started. God, what a job!
Harding, in office

Are you certain that you [John F Kennedy] are quite ready or that the country is quite ready for you in the role of President in 1961? I am greatly concerned and troubled about the situation we are up against in the world now and in the immediate future. That is why I would hope that someone with the greatest possible maturity and experience will be available by this time.
Former (Democratic) **President Truman** shortly before the Democratic Party convention, July 1960

His [Kennedy's] record ... is ... good enough for me.
Truman, campaigning, October 1960

When I make statements, I stick by them.
Truman, campaigning, two days later

The inescapable and harmful by-product of such operations as Social Security ... has been the weakening of the individual personality and of self-reliance.

US senator **Barry Goldwater**, 1956

Let me say for perhaps the one millionth time, lest there be any doubt in anyone's mind – that I support the Social Security system and I want to see it strengthened.

Goldwater, as Republican candidate, presidential election campaign, 1964

I have here in my hand a list of 205 ... members of the Communist Party and who, nevertheless are still working and shaping policy in the State Department.

Senator Joseph McCarthy, Senate speech initiating his anti-Communist witchhunt which would transfix America for four years at the height of the Cold War, February 1950. The campaign was characterized by whipped-up paranoia and 'guilt by association' tactics, and little actual proof.

[This is] a conspiracy of infamy so black that, when it is finally exposed, its principals shall be for ever deserving of the maledictions of all honest men.

McCarthy, speech, Senate June 1951

I think it is a shoddy, unusual thing to do to use the floor of the Senate to attack your opponent without any proof whatever.

McCarthy, complaining against attacks on him in the Senate, 1956

It is an unfortunate fact that we can secure peace only by preparing for war.

President John F Kennedy, 1960

We will not act prematurely or unecessarily risk the costs of world-wide nuclear war in which even the fruits of victory would be ashes in our mouth. But neither will we shrink from that risk at any time it must be faced.

Kennedy, 1962

The basic problems facing the world today are not susceptible to a military solution.

Kennedy

I also believe that academic freedom should protect the right of a professor or student to advocate Marxism, Socialism, Communism or any other minority viewpoint – no matter how distasteful to the majority.

Richard Nixon

What are our schools for if not indoctrination against Communism?

Nixon

A government makes no more fateful decision than the decision to go to war. The President should want to share that decision with Congress.

Warren Christopher, US Secretary of State, on the President's right to decide whether to send US troops into battle, 1982

We can't tie the hands of the President.

Christopher, responding to Congress's wish to be involved in decisions on sending troops to Bosnia, September 1994

Bob says he offers real leadership – he's right, backwards not forwards.

Jack Kemp, running against George Bush and Bob Dole for the Republican presidential nomination, 1988

The candidate of pain, austerity and sacrifice.

Kemp, on Dole, 1988

He has never met a tax he hasn't hiked.

Kemp, on Dole, 1988

When he talks about the future, I'm sure it is time to grab your wallets. I am convinced that Senator Dole has a secret plan to raise taxes on the American people.

Kemp, on Dole, 1988

When his library burned down, it destroyed both books. Dole hadn't finished colouring the second.

Kemp, on Dole

It is the greatest honor of my life to have been asked to run by the greatest American hero.

Kemp, accepting Dole's invitation to be his running mate, presidential campaigns, August 1996

I can't wait to make the case for Bob Dole in every community and every neighbourhood of the United States of America. Our country needs a leader whose stature is equal to that calling, and it's Bob Dole.

Kemp, acceptance speech, August 1996

We need someone who will fight for his principles, who loves America, knows what it means to sacrifice for others, to sacrifice for his nation, to demonstrate courage under fire ... Bob Dole is that man.

Kemp, acceptance speech, August 1996

When he was a quarterback, he played without a helmet.

Bob Dole's previous outlook on Kemp

I never want to speak to that man again.

Dole, after Kemp withdrew from the primary campaign and publicly endorsed rival Steve Forbes, April 1996.

6 *Ahem*

I May Have Misled You

Intentions change. Though consistency of purpose is
thought a virtue in public life, those who lead often find
that the first draft of their plans later requires a little tweak
here and there. Sometimes, they were lying first time;
sometimes they really meant it ...

Read my lips. No new taxes.

George Bush, presidential campaign, 1988. (He won – then raised them a
year later, with the second biggest tax rise in American history.) His son,
George W Bush, pledged not to raise taxes when he ran for governor of
Texas in 1994. He asked voters to 'Read my ears'. He also won.

We don't need quick political promises out in a parking lot somewhere,
to be forgotten when the election's over.

Bush, campaign, 1988

We raised taxes on the American people and we put this country right
into a recession.

Dan Quayle, apologizing for President Bush's 'no new taxes' pledge,
September 1992

The government have no plans to extend the scope of VAT to any items which are currently zero-rated and have no need to do so.

John Major, House of Commons, 9 March 1992

We have no plans to widen the scope of VAT.

Major, general election press conference, March 1992

I propose over the next two years to end the zero rate of VAT on fuel and power ... VAT will be charged at 8 per cent from 1 April 1994 and 17.5 per cent from 1 April 1995.

Norman Lamont, Chancellor of the Exchequer, Budget statement, March 1993, announcing the imposition of VAT on domestic gas, electricity and coal

We want no wars of conquest. We must avoid the temptation of territorial aggression.

President William McKinley, inaugural address, 1897. In his four years of office, the United States invaded and occupied Cuba, seized Puerto Rico, Guam and the Philippines, and annexed Hawaii in the largest overseas expansion of American territorial interests in its history.

Forceful intervention in Chechnya is unacceptable. If we violate this principle, the Caucasus will rise up. There will be so much terror and blood that afterwards no one will forgive us.

Boris Yeltsin, Russian President, August 1994. Four months later, he ordered Russian troops into Chechnya. To date, an estimated 30,000 civilians have died in the war.

The military phase of the Chechen campaign is effectively over.

Boris Yeltsin, after Russian troops captured the Chechen parliament building, January 1995. A vicious guerrilla war ensued.

I fight on. I fight to win.

Margaret Thatcher, after failing to win the required majority in the first round of the Conservative Party leadership contest, 21 November 1990

I have concluded that the unity of the party and the prospects of victory in a general election would be better served if I stood down.

Thatcher, withdrawing from the leadership contest, 22 November 1990

This is not a lightly given pledge. It is a promise. We shall achieve the 500,000 target, and we shall not allow any developments, any circumstances, however adverse, to deflect us from our aim.

Harold Wilson, Prime Minister, on Labour's programme of council house building, general election campaign, March 1966. The government was to fall short of that figure by 100,000

There are too many uncertainties for it to be possible for anyone to say exactly how many will be built.

Anthony Greenwood, Wilson's Minister of Housing, abandoning the government's target, January 1968

There was no impropriety whatsoever in my acquaintanceship with Miss Keeler. ... I shall not hesitate to issue writs for libel and slander if scandalous allegations are made or repeated outside the House.

John Profumo, Secretary of State for War, statement in the House of Commons, March 1963

In my statement I said that there had been no impropriety in this association. To my very deep regret I have to admit that this is not true, and that I misled you and my colleagues, and the House.

Profumo, resignation letter to Prime Minister Harold Macmillan, June 1963. (It prompted the doggerel:

'What have you done?' cried Christine,
'You've wrecked the whole party machine.
To lie in nude may be rude,
But to lie in the House is obscene.')

My colleagues and I will never use words or support actions which exploit or intensify divisions in our society.

Edward Heath, on becoming Prime Minister, June 1970. In October he published plans for reform of the trade unions, culminating in the 1971 Industrial Relations Act, which was bitterly opposed by the unions. In July he had opened negotiations for Britain's entry into the EEC, which polarized most of the rest of the country.

A social democratic party without deep roots in the working class movement would quickly fade into an unrepresentative intellectual sect.

Roy Jenkins, 1972

The Labour Party is and always has been an instinctive part of my life.

Jenkins, 1973

There is a lot of talk about a centre party – and that I might lead it. I find this idea profoundly unattractive.

Jenkins, 1973

If I got fed up with the Labour Party, I should leave politics altogether.

Shirley Williams, 1979

We believe that a centre party would have no roots, no principles, no philosophy, and no values.

Williams, 1980

I would not join a centre party because I feel the whole idea is wrong.
Williams, 1980

There is no way I could have been anything but a socialist. It would have been a clear revolt against my whole upbringing and family background.
Williams, 1980. A year later she was a founder of the SDP.

We are the heart of the party. We are what the Labour movement is all about. We are going to win and we are going to keep it that way.
William Rodgers, on being a Labour moderate, 1977. In 1981 he was one of the 'Gang of Four' founders of the SDP. So were Williams and Jenkins

Our acts must be guided by one single, hard-headed thought: keeping America out of this war.
US President Franklin Roosevelt, September 1939

We are keeping out of the wars that are going on in Europe and Asia.
Roosevelt, April 1940

We will not send our men to take part in European wars.
Roosevelt, July 1940

And while I am talking to you mothers and fathers, I give you one more assurance. I have said this before, but I shall say it again and again and again: Your boys are not going to be sent into any foreign wars.
Roosevelt, October 1940

The [Cuban] movement is not a Communist movement ... We have no intention of expropriating US property.

Fidel Castro, visiting Washington 'as a good neighbour' shortly after taking power in 1959, declaring his wish to allay fears about his new regime. By 1961 the new government had expropriated over $1 billion of US property.

I am a Marxist-Leninist and will be one until the day I die.

Castro, December 1961

We have to be ready to conduct the necessary reforms to adapt our country and our economy to the present world situation.

Castro, January 1995

We shall never stop until we can go back home and Israel is destroyed. The goal of our struggle is the end of Israel and there can be no compromises or mediations.

Yasser Arafat, Palestinian leader, 1970

Mr Prime Minister ... the PLO recognizes the right of Israel to exist in peace and security [and] renounces the use of terrorism and other acts of violence.

Arafat, signing the Middle East peace deal with Israel at the White House, September 1993

You have come to fight and start a *jihad* to liberate Jerusalem, the historic shrine.

Arafat addressing mosque worshippers during a visit to South Africa in the middle of peace negotiations with Israel, May 1994. He later claimed that *jihad* – holy war – was to be construed as the battle for peace.

I will never, ever agree to a halfway effort.

President George Bush, nationwide broadcast on the Allied military build-up in the Gulf in response to the Iraqi invasion of Kuwait, a month before unleashing the Desert Storm operation, December 1990. It stopped half way

It seems to me that Saddam cannot survive … people are fed up with him. They see him for the brutal dictator he is.

Bush, predicting the imminent demise of Saddam Hussein's regime in Iraq, three weeks after its military defeat in the Gulf War, March 1991

I miscalculated.

Bush, five years after his Gulf War prediction that allied military victory would topple Saddam Hussein, January 1996

Britain's frontiers are on the Himalayas.

Harold Wilson, Prime Minister, defining Britain's security perspective, 1965

We have no intention of ratting on any of our commitments. We intend to remain and still remain fully capable of carrying out all the commitments we have at the present time, including the Far East, the Middle East and Africa. We do intend to remain in every sense a world power.

Denis Healey, Defence Secretary, 1966.

We intend to make to the alliances of which we are members a contribution related to our economic capability while recognizing that our security lies fundamentally in Europe and must be based on the North Atlantic alliance.

Harold Wilson, statement to the House of Commons, January 1968 announcing the withdrawal of a military presence East of Suez from 1971

The essential feature of our current defence policy is a readiness to recognize that political and economic realities reinforce the defence arguments for concentrating Britain's military role in Europe.

Wilson's Defence White Paper, February 1969

Should I become President I will not risk American lives by permitting any other nation to drag us into the wrong war at the wrong place at the wrong time through an unwise commitment that is unwise militarily, unnecessary to our security, and unsupported by our allies.

John F Kennedy, presidential campaign, October 1960. At the time, America's involvement in Vietnam consisted of 700 military advisers.

If necessary I would consider the use of US forces to help South Vietnam resist Communist pressures.

Kennedy, now President, press conference, May 1961. By early 1962, there were 4,000 military 'advisers'; by the end of the year, 12,000. When Kennedy was assasssinated, there were 16,000 committed.

We Americans know ... the risks of spreading conflict. We still seek no wider war.

President Lyndon Johnson, August 1964

We are not about to send American boys nine or ten thousand miles away from home to do what Asian boys ought to be doing for themselves.

Johnson, election speech, October 1964. The first US ground troops went into Vietnam the following March. By the end of 1965 there were 185,000, reaching at their peak (1969) over half a million.

There is and will be, as long as I am President, peace for all Americans.

Johnson, October 1964

Let every nation know ... we shall pay any price, bear any burden, meet any hardship, support any friend, oppose any foe to assure the survival and the success of liberty.

President John Kennedy, inaugural address, 1961

America cannot – and will not – conceive all the plans, design all the programmes, execute all the decisions and undertake all the defence of the free nations of the world.

Richard Nixon, presidential address to Congress, February 1970. He was to end the war

The Germans, if this government is returned, are going to pay every penny; they are going to be squeezed, as a lemon is squeezed – until the pips squeak.

Sir Eric Geddes, First Lord of the Admiralty, general election campaign, December 1918, immediately after the First World War. Germany eventually paid one-eighth of the sum originally demanded.

I would flatly oppose any grant by the federal government to all states in the Union for educational purposes.

Dwight Eisenhower, 1949

The federal government should serve as an effective agent in dealing with this [classroom shortage] problem.

Eisenhower, now President, State of the Union address, 1955

The federal government contributes to economic growth when it takes its part ... in providing public facilities such as ... educational institutions.

Eisenhower, 1955

I don't believe myself it is necessary for the people as a whole to have their living standards lowered in order to conquer inflation.

Denis Healey, Chancellor of the Exchequer, election campaign, September 1974

If we tighten our belts now we can start moving ahead next year and we'll be in far better shape then than at any time since the war.

Healey, Budget broadcast, April 1975

I do not think that this would be the right moment to cut people's standard of life in terms of private consumption any further.

James Callaghan, Prime Minister, House of Commons, July 1976

Let me say that of course there has been a fall in people's standard of life. And it has fallen this year and will fall again next year.

Callaghan, BBC TV, October 1976

The standard of living has been deliberately reduced by the government over the last eighteen months in order that we should get ourselves financially straight again. That should be a matter for congratulation and not for recrimination.

Denis Healey, interview with ABC TV, March 1977

My administration will work very closely with you to bring about a spirit of co-operation between the President and the air traffic controllers.

Ronald Reagan, letter to Air Traffic Controllers' Union president, election campaign, October 1980. When the controllers went on strike in 1981, Reagan sacked them all.

The Labour Party gives defence of the pound the first priority. We shall need to sacrifice all other considerations to make sterling strong.

Harold Wilson, shadow Chancellor, February 1958

Devaluation would be regarded all over the world as an acknowledgement of defeat, a recognition that we are not on a springboard, but a slide.

Wilson, July 1961

Devaluation, whether of sterling, or of the dollar, or both, would be a lunatic, self-destroying operation.

Wilson, Opposition leader, 1963

The facilities for further borrowing which have been ... built up these past few years have given us a firm base from which we can advance without panic measures, without devaluation, without stop-and-go measures.

Wilson, October 1964. Over the next six years Britain had them all.

From now the pound abroad is worth 14 per cent or so less in terms of other currencies. It does not mean, of course, that the pound here in Britain, in your pocket or purse, or in your bank has been devalued.

Wilson, television statement announcing devaluation, 1967

I will say then that I am not, nor ever have been in favour of bringing about in any way the social and political equality of the white and black races ... There is a physical difference between the white and black races which I believe will for ever forbid the two races living together on terms of social and political equality. And inasmuch as they cannot so live, while they do remain together there must be the position of superior and inferior, and I as much as any other man am in favour of having the superior position assigned to the white race.

Abraham Lincoln, campaigning for the Senate, August 1858

Even when you cease to be slaves, you are yet far removed from being placed on an equality with the white race. You are cut off from many of the advantages which the other race enjoys. It is better for us both to be separated.

Lincoln, then President, during a meeting with free Negro leaders, White House, August 1862

If my name ever goes into history, it will be for this act, and my whole soul is in it.

Lincoln, signing the Emancipation Proclamation, ending slavery in the United States, January 1863

The central act of my administration, and the great event of the nine-teenth century. ... It is a momentous thing to be the instrument ... of the liberation of a race.

Lincoln, describing the Emancipation Proclamation, 1863

We are determined not to put these gains in peril through allowing vital decisions on great issues of national economic policy to be transferred from the British Parliament at Westminster to some supra-national European assembly ... We intend to hold what we have gained here in this island.

Hugh Dalton, former Chancellor of the Exchequer, stating the Labour government's opposition to European economic integration – on the grounds it would overturn Labour's achievements at home, Labour Party conference, 1950

We have not successfully rolled back the frontiers of the state in Britain only to see them reimposed at a European level, with a European super-state exercising a new dominance from Brussels.

Margaret Thatcher, opposing closer European economic integration – on the grounds it would overturn Conservative achievements at home, speech at Bruges, September 1988

We've got a big job to do in some of those inner cities, a really big job. Our policies are geared – education and housing – to help people in the inner cities ...

Thatcher, victory speech inside No 10, election night, June 1987

It would be quite wrong to indicate that there is a pot of gold and all you have to do is say 'Please, I want more [for the inner cities].'

Thatcher, September 1987

I don't think that anyone actually wants that to be a priority of the Labour Party at the moment ... I don't think anyone is saying now ... that this is the sort of thing we should focus on.

Tony Blair, asked whether he opposed the dropping of Labour's historic Clause Four on nationalization, during the party leadership campaign, June 1994. After becoming leader the following month, he announced the review of Clause Four at the party conference in September leading a successful high-profile campaign in 1995 for its scrapping.

Yes, I support repeal of the ban on gays and lesbians serving in the United States armed forces.

Bill Clinton, presidential campaign, 1992

I intend to keep my commitment.

Clinton, five days after his inauguration as President, January 1993

I do not propose any changes in the code of military conduct. None. Zero. I do not believe that anything should be done in terms of behaviour that would undermine unit cohesion or morale.

Clinton, Cleveland press club, May 1993

I do not think we should ever pick a fight with the President of the United States if it's avoidable.

Newt Gingrich, Speaker of the US House of Representatives, December 1994. He was later blamed for unnecessarily prolonging the 1995 budget settlement in retaliation for not being allowed to sit at the front of an aircraft with Bill Clinton when they travelled together to the funeral of assassinated Israeli Prime Minister Yitzhak Rabin, November 1995

Which of the two of us do you think cares more about the government not showing up. Him or me?

Gingrich, provoking a second shutdown of the American federal services because of failure to settle the budget, January 1996

As to the idea of freezing wages ... I think this would be monstrously unfair ... I do not think you could ever legislate for wage increases, and no party is setting out to do that.

Harold Wilson, March 1966. Four months later, he introduced a wage freeze.

I see no need for a Royal Commission [on trade unions] which would take minutes and waste years.

Wilson, September 1964. He announced one six months later.

I have often been accused of putting my foot in my mouth, but I have never put my hand in your pocket.

Spiro Agnew, Richard Nixon's Vice-President, 1969–73

Criminal elements ... are truly the enemies of our country. ... They weaken its economy by infiltrating legitimate businesses ... by cheating on taxes, and by other frauds. These then are the enemy: the organized criminal ... the tax cheat, the embezzler ... the dishonest businessman. Like all who threaten the life and health of the nation, they must be fought with every weapon available.

Agnew, June 1970. He resigned in 1973 pleading 'no contest' to charges of bribery, extortion and tax fraud involving contracts going back ten years to his time as Governor of Maryland and continuing when he became Vice-President. The court document listing the charges ran to forty pages

After all, what does a politician have but credibility?

Agnew

We intend to play the ball, not the man ...

Harold Wilson, disclaiming interest in who would win the leadership
contest in the Conservative Party, October 1963

After half a century of democratic advance, the whole process has
ground to a halt with a 14th Earl.

Wilson, playing the man, on the success of Lord Home, October 1963.
Home renounced his earldom two days later to become Sir Alec Douglas-
Home and become eligible for a seat in the Commons.

I suppose Mr Wilson, when you come to think of it, is the 14th Mr
Wilson.

Lord Home, in response

7 *Moi?*

Ambitions Disavowed

No politician ever covets the top job. Heaven forbid. They seek only to serve. Ambition is alien to their natures. However, under intense and unremitting pressure from their friends, and more out of courtesy than desire, some do finally fail to prevent their names going forward. It seems that, from a notionally vast choice of possible candidates, we end up being governed by one or another of a small group whose firm intention it was that the job should never be theirs ...

I do not think I shall be tempted to quit this agreeable residence ... the great object of my political career is now achieved.

Benjamin Disraeli, in Paris watching the fall of Sir Robert Peel, Disraeli's arch political foe, December 1845

I declare unequivocally, I will not accept the vice-presidential nomination.

George Bush, running for nomination as the Republican presidential candidate, 1980. He lost to Ronald Reagan, and became Reagan's running mate.

I could never be Prime Minister. I do my sums with matchsticks.

Lord Home, 1962

I would rather die than serve under Lloyd George.

Lord Curzon, Asquith's Lord Privy Seal, 4 December 1916, during Lloyd George's manoeuvrings to force Asquith's resignation because of his handling of the First World War. Asquith quit on 5 December; Curzon accepted the post of Lord President of the Council when Lloyd George became Prime Minister on 7 December, and served throughout the six years of the premiership.

There is nothing I want so much as an opportunity to retire.

Dwight D Eisenhower, when allied military commander, 1945

In the strongest language you can command, you may say that I have no political ambitions at all. Make it even stronger than that if you wish.

Eisenhower, to his press staff, 1945.

My decision to remove myself completely from the political scene is definite and positive.

Eisenhower, ruling himself out of contention for political office, 1948

Under no circumstances will I ask for relief from this assignment in order to seek nomination to public office.

Eisenhower, 1952, when supreme commander of NATO. Two months later he announced he would stand for the Presidency that year, and won.

If I ever show any interest in yielding to persuasion, please call in the psychiatrists, or even better, the sheriff. I feel that there can be no showing made that my duty extends beyond a one-term performance.

Eisenhower, 1953, shortly after election. He ran for, and won, a second term in 1956.

I promise Patricia Ryan Nixon that I will not again seek public office.

Richard Nixon to his wife, 1952. Later the same year he was elected as Eisenhower's Vice-President.

I say categorically that I have no contemplation at all of being the candidate for anything in 1964, 1966, 1968 or 1972. Anybody who thinks I would be a candidate for anything in any year is off his rocker.

Nixon, 1963. He ran for, and won, the presidential election in 1968, and retained office in the 1972 election.

Of all the men running, Richard Nixon is the most dangerous to have as President. I would never work for that man. That man is a disaster.

Henry Kissinger, during election campaign, 1968. He served throughout the Nixon presidency, as National Security Adviser and, from 1973, as Secretary of State.

I don't think anybody from the South will be nominated [for President] in my lifetime. If so, I don't think he will be elected.

Senator Lyndon Baines Johnson, a Texan, 1958. He became President in 1963 after Kennedy's assassination, and was elected in his own right in 1964.

I will never, never trade my Senate seat for the vice-presidency.

Johnson, who became John Kennedy's vice-presidential running mate in 1960

The governor has asked me to reiterate what he has said on many occasions – he is not a candidate for President or any other national office.

Ronald Reagan's press officer, 1969

The thought of being President frightens me and I do not think I want the job.

Reagan, Governor of California, 1973

I'd rather bungee jump without the cord.

Ross Perot, unsuccessful third candidate in the 1992 presidential election, asked in April 1993 whether he intended to run again in 1996

We have to be responsive to the people who created this party, and they have a strong desire for me to participate ... I will continue to make whatever sacrifice is necessary.

Perot, announcing his intention to run as the Reform Party candidate, July 1996

Knowing full well the responsibilities that devolve on a Prime Minister, and how difficult it is to cater to all requirements of a nation and satisfy them, I will not accept the post of Premier even if it is offered me.

Mrs Sirimavo Bandaranaike of Ceylon, 1958. She became the world's first woman Prime Minister in 1960.

I can tell you absolutely, certainly that at the next election, when my term runs out, I am not going to be in the running.

Boris Yeltsin, ruling himself out of seeking re-election in 1996, June 1992

My departure ... would be an irresponsible and irreparably mistaken step. ... I am convinced that I can lead this country out of confusion, anxiety and uncertainty.

Yeltsin, announcing his intention to stand for re-election as President, February 1996

My position on the third term is perfectly simple. I said I would not accept a nomination for a third term under any circumstances, meaning of course a third consecutive term.

Theodore Roosevelt, elaborating his decision to enter the 1912 campaign, after his 1904 announcement that he wouldn't go for a third term

No woman in my time will be Prime Minister or Foreign Secretary – not the top jobs. Anyway, I wouldn't want to be Prime Minister. You have to give yourself one hundred per cent.

Margaret Thatcher, *Sunday Telegraph*, 1969

It will be years before a woman either leads the [Conservative] Party or becomes Prime Minister. I don't see it happening in my time.

Thatcher, June 1974

I don't want to be leader of the party – I'm happy to be in the top dozen.

Thatcher, 1974

At various times in the next twenty or thirty years I think it is reasonable to anticipate that I will be among the leadership of the Labour Party, but as for being leader, I can't see it happening, and I'm not particularly keen on it happening.

Neil Kinnock, 1981. He became Leader in October 1983.

I have ten more years of active life. I have other ideas for them.

Douglas Hurd, Foreign Secretary, ruling himself out when asked if he planned to stand for the Conservative Party leadership, October 1990. The following month he stood.

I have made my position clear. I am not going to take part in that process. I think that Mrs Thatcher will lead the Conservative Party into the next election and that she will win it.

Michael Heseltine, asked whether he would stand in a leadership contest, October 1990

The opinion polls now say that I am best placed to recover those people who have indicated that without a change of leader they will not vote Conservative at the next election ... Geoffrey Howe's resignation revealed divisions which would not go away without a contest of this sort.

Heseltine, announcing his candidature for the leadership, November 1990

As far as I am concerned, the opening bat is well played in and will stay there for some years to come.

John Major, ruling himself out of a leadership contest, October 1990

To offer myself as a candidate for President requires ... a passion and commitment that, despite my every effort, I do not have for political life.

General Colin Powell, announcing his decision not to run, November 1995

Only stupid people don't change their minds.

Boutros Boutros-Ghali, UN Secretary-General, announcing that he might seek a second term of office in 1998 after pledging to serve just one when he took the post in 1992, May 1994. He confirmed his intention to run in June 1996.

If they give me the old heave-ho, I would not want to represent any other seat. I have fallen in love with Bath. I have tried to be honest and avoid the political ping-pong. If voters don't want that I'm not sure I want to stay in politics at all.

Chris Patten, campaigning, speaking to the *Bath & West Evening Chronicle*, 3 February 1982.

What I know is that I shall only ever be the Member of Parliament for Bath. No Plumshire North for me.

Chris Patten, writing in an outline 'Why I ❤ Bath' for the *Bath & West Evening Chronicle*, 22 April 1988

I couldn't simply transfer to some other constituency straight away. In the long term, who knows? But I do not regard the constituency for which you have worked as being like an off-the-peg suit to be put on and then discarded.

Chris Patten, reflecting on his defeat to the *Bath &West Eveing Chronicle*, 25 April 1992

Watch this space ...

8 *Oh!*

Sheer Bloody Nerve

'Oh!' is Hansard's notation for MPs' squeals of outrage at a shocking impertinence; but balls, a brass neck, a thick skin and acres of cheek are among the qualifications for high office. Statements which may be downright arrogant, unbelievably insensitive or perfectly preposterous are routine. For brazen effrontery, Catherine the Great takes the biscuit – and runs with it in the relay which follows …

I shall be an autocrat: that's my trade. And the good Lord will forgive me: that's his.

Catherine II (the Great), Empress of Russia 1762–96 (attrib.)

An extraordinary affair. I gave them their orders and they wanted to stay and discuss them.

Duke of Wellington, description of his first Cabinet as Prime Minister, 1828

Why has Jesus Christ so far not succeeded in inducing the world to follow his teachings? It is because He taught the ideal without devising any practical means of attaining it. That is why I am proposing a practical scheme to carry out His aims.

President Woodrow Wilson, setting himself modest ambitions for the post-First World War world, Versailles Peace Conference, 1919

We went into West Beirut in order to guarantee it, not to control it. We went in to prevent bloodshed, to prevent anarchy.

Ben Meir, deputy Prime Minister of Israel, on the Israeli invasion of Lebanon in 1982. An estimated 18,000 people died and 30,000 were injured, 90 per cent of them civilians, including over 1,000 in a massacre at two Palestinian refugee camps in the city.

From the Israeli point of view, it is the most humane siege of a city imaginable.

Izchak Ben-Ari, Israeli ambassador to Germany, on the invasion of Beirut, 1982

Whenever you accept our views, we shall be in full agreement with you.

General Moshe Dayan, Israeli Foreign Minister to US Secretary of State Cyrus Vance during Arab–Israeli peace talks, August 1977

I am proud of democracy in the country and do not want to do anything against it.

Indian Prime Minister **Indira Gandhi**, July 1975. The previous month she had responded to a High Court ruling declaring her 1971 election null and void by arresting 676 opposition leaders, postponing elections due in 1976, changing the electoral law to nullify the court judgement against her. She then ruled under a national State of Emergency for twenty-one months.

We're the most democratic country in Latin America.

Fidel Castro, Cuban leader, July 1991

Law 5: All repressive laws shall be repealed. Law 6: Drinking, adultery, obscenity, gambling, and other immoral practices shall be banned.

From the manifesto of the Muslim resistance in Afghanistan announcing a list of new laws to be introduced if it defeated occupying Soviet forces, 1981

In view of the success of my economic revolution in Uganda, I offer myself to be appointed Head of the Commonwealth.

Ugandan President **Idi Amin**, 1975

If I was there for several terms of office, it wasn't because I wanted to be. It was because the people insisted.

Alfredo Stroessner, Paraguayan dictator accounting for his thirty-five years as President, in which he orchestrated seven fraudulent re-elections, April 1990

At least I left shoes in my closets and not skeletons. And besides, I didn't have 3,000 pairs of shoes. I only had 1,060.

Imelda Marcos, 1987

I was never attached to power or valuables. I have no attachment to worldly things.

Marcos, about to return to the Philippines from exile in Hawaii to face charges that she and her late husband President Ferdinand Marcos salted away $2 billion from the state treasury, October 1991

People tell me I live in a mansion here, but I tell them I used to live in a palace. It's all relative.

Marcos, on life in exile in Hawaii, September 1989

Writers are much more esteemed here; they play a much larger part in society than they do in the West ... the advantage of not being free is that people do listen to you.

Lord Snow, being interviewed on Radio Moscow, 1971

I am not and have never been a man of the right. My position was on the left and is now in the centre of politics.

Oswald Mosley, British fascist leader in the 1930s, letter to *The Times*, 1968

Socialism is what a Labour government does.

Herbert Morrison, Labour deputy Prime Minister under Attlee, 1945–51

In the case of nutrition and health, just as in the case of education, the gentlemen in Whitehall really do know better what is good for the people than the people know themselves.

Douglas Jay, Labour ideologist and future Labour Treasury and Trade Minister, in *The Socialist Case*, 1937

I took part in the Grunwick picket line ... I joined in because I thought my union, APEX, was perfectly right on the merits of the dispute.

Shirley Williams, Paymaster General in the Labour government, 1977

Well, I wasn't part of the picket line. I visited those who were picketing.

Williams, general election campaign (in which she lost her seat), 1979

Inflation ... is currently running at 8.4 per cent.

Denis Healey, Chancellor of the Exchequer, press conference, September 1974, at the start of the general election campaign. The claim was notorious for its inaccuracy: the actual rate was later shown to be 15.6 per cent.

People who start things don't often see the end of them – take Moses and the Promised Land.

Margaret Thatcher, reflecting with characteristic modesty on her premiership, 1992

We are in the fortunate position, in Britain, of being, as it were, the senior person in power.

Thatcher to a reporter *en route* to Moscow, 1987

I want them to have the courage of *my* convictions.

Thatcher, asked by an interviewer whether she respected independent-minded Cabinet colleagues who had the courage of their convictions

I rate myself a deeply committed pacifist.

Richard Nixon, 1971

Wherever any … father talks to his child, I hope he can look at the man in the White House and, whatever he may think of his politics, he will say: 'Well, there is a man who maintains the kind of standards personally that I would want my child to follow.'

Nixon, TV debate with John Kennedy, presidential campaign, 1960

Let us begin by committing ourselves to the truth, to see it like it is and to tell it like it is, to find the truth, to speak the truth and live with the truth. That's what we'll do.

Nixon, accepting the Republican presidential nomination, 1968

Now the purists probably won't agree with [the break-in], but I don't think you're going to see a great, great uproar in the country.

Nixon, to his aides four days after the Watergate break-in, June 1972, taped conversation released in 1993

The White House has had no involvement whatever in this particular incident.

Nixon, first public comment on the Watergate break-in, five days after the event, June 1972

I don't give a shit what happens. I want you all to stonewall it. Let them plead the Fifth Amendment, cover up, or anything else if it'll save the plan.

Nixon, White House tapes, on obstructing the Watergate investigations, March 1973

There can be no whitewash at the White House.

Nixon, address to the nation after sacking four of his most senior aides whom he sought to make responsible for the Watergate cover-up, April 1973

I reject the cynical view that politics is inevitably or even usually a dirty business.

Nixon, same address, April 1973

I want these to be the best days in American history.

Nixon, concluding the address, referring to the 1,361 days remaining in his presidency, April 1973

I am convinced that we are going to make it the whole road and put this thing in the funny pages of the history books.

John Dean, counsellor to Richard Nixon, reassuring the President on the forthcoming Senate investigation into Watergate, 1973

Watergate is water under the bridge.

Richard Nixon, September 1973

I've got what it takes to stay.

Nixon, November 1973

I do not expect to be impeached, and I will not resign.

Nixon, February 1974

I let down my friends. I let down my country. I let down our system of government.

Nixon, 1977

We did not – repeat – did not trade weapons or anything else for hostages – nor will we.

Ronald Reagan, national TV broadcast, denying allegations of arms sales to Iran in return for the release of American hostages held in Lebanon, 13 November 1986. Six days later he admitted there had been a deal.

I did not approve the arms trade.

Reagan, 11 February 1987

I don't remember – period.

Reagan, questioned about his involvement, 20 February 1987

I don't recall.

Ed Meese, Attorney General and close Reagan confidant, testifying to the Congressional Iran-Contra hearings, 1987. He used this, or similar phrases, 187 times.

A few months ago I told the American people I did not trade arms for hostages. My heart and my best intentions still tell me that is true, but the facts and the evidence tell me it is not.

Ronald Reagan, correcting his earlier denial of involvement in selling arms to Iran in return for the release of American hostages held in Lebanon, March 1987

I can assure the House nothing of the kind ever occurred. I never shall – it is totally foreign to my nature – make any application for any place … I never directly or indirectly solicited office.

Benjamin Disraeli, lying to the House of Commons, 1846, after his speech criticizing Prime Minister Peel's fitness for office. Peel had immediately retaliated by asking, if that was the case, why Disraeli had asked him for a post in his government. Disraeli had indeed written to Peel in 1841 begging for office. His luck held – Peel could not find the letter to prove it until years later.

Son, they're *all* my helicopters.

President Johnson, on a visit to a military base, to the officer who had directed him with the words, 'That's your helicopter over there, sir.'

They should've prayed too.

Rev. Pat Robertson, religious-right US presidential candidate 1988, reminded of his admission that in 1978 he prayed that an impending hurricane would not hit his television station. It hit somewhere else, and killed several people.

The difference between rape and seduction is salesmanship.

Bill Carpenter, Mayor of Independence, Missouri, 1990

It is the normal British practice for the wife to go where her husband desires.

Ivor Stanbrook MP, *Today*, BBC Radio, 1982

You can't have a race living here for 70,000 years without leaving some of their debris about. In another 70,000 years you will be able to see our beer cans, won't you, as a sign of our culture.

Australian Minister for Conservation, on Aboriginal artefacts, 1981

We took a considered decision to trade up to something better ... I haven't heard from Buckingham Palace ... She hasn't rung.

Paul Keating, Australian Prime Minister, on his republican policy, 1996

Would they be cutting high tax rates in India today, if we had not first done it here?

Mr Major, speech 14 March 1992

Would they be privatising in Latin America today, if we hadn't first done it here?

Major, speech, 14 March 1992

I think and hope that we have conveyed not merely the impression, but the conviction that, whatever other countries or governments may do, the British government is never untrue to its word, and is never disloyal to its colleagues or its allies, never does anything underhand or mean; and if this conviction be widespread – as I believe it to be – that is the real basis of the moral authority which the British Empire has long exerted and I believe will long continue to exert in the affairs of mankind.

Lord Curzon, Foreign Secretary, 1923

9 *Uh?*

You Cannot be Serious

Beneath the daily ebb and flow of opinion, fortune and political fashion, there are more powerful currents at work. Historic shifts are as gradual as they are finally huge, leaving the certainties of other ages looking astonishingly idiotic. But it is important to remember that, though some of the opinions expressed below were controversial even at the time, few will have seemed absurd. The arguments which follow are from past Members of Parliament as recorded by Hansard. Impossible though it would be to advance them seriously at a modern dinner party, you may react to a few with a sneaking sympathy. You may even sympathise with a few of our ancestors' forebodings about the likely consequences of new inventions. While laughing at what they thought, ask yourself at which of our own assumptions our successors may laugh ...

The slave trade

It is absurd to suppose that the merchants whose profit arises from the number of healthy Africans they land in the West India islands would not attend to their own interests and take every possible care to preserve their health.

Lord Rodney, 1788

I acknowledge it is not an amiable trade but neither is the trade of a butcher an amiable trade and yet a mutton chop is, nevertheless, a very good thing ... I think we should not too curiously inquire into the unpleasant circumstances with which [the slave trade] is perhaps attended.

Mr Grosvenor, 1791

[Abolition] will terminate all spirit of adventure, all incitement to industry, all thirst of emulation, for hitherto it has been the hope of overseers to rise in the world as soon as they had obtained that employment, and the means they had of doing so was by saving a portion of their wages to purchase two or three Negroes which they let out ... for hire.

Sir William Young, 1796

The slave trade [has] promote[d] the cause of humanity, for it can hardly be doubted that ... prisoners would have shared the same fate as the other [dead warriors] if avarice had not prevailed over revenge in the mind of the savage king.

Mr Edwards, citing the practice of African kings selling prisoners of war to slave traders instead of imposing the usual fate of execution, 1798

The abolition of the slave trade would cause many Africans to be murdered since there would be no sale for the prisoners of war.

Mr Thornton, 1798

The slave trade tends in a very considerable degree to lessen this waste of human blood ... [slaves] are conveyed from a country of barbarous superstition to a land of civilization and humanity. In my opinion, therefore, the clamours against the trade are groundless.

Mr Henniker Major, 1798

The abolition of the slave trade would be the scourge of Africa ... I desire its continuance out of humanity to the inhabitants of the coast of Africa.

Mr Petrie, 1799

The Africans are accustomed to slavery in their own country and the taking of them to another quarter of the globe is therefore no great hardship.

Sir William Young, 1804

The state of slaves in Africa is truly deplorable and therefore taking them away, particularly to the English colonies, is a relief to them.

Mr Fuller, 1804

It is not at all clear that it is just for the mother country to treat the colonies in the way she has, first by giving ... encouragement to the traffic in question and afterwards, when large properties had been embarked in them, endeavouring thus to put a stop to it and thereby involving in beggary and ruin those who have risked their property and thereby added greatly to the wealth, prosperity and aggrandizement of the whole Empire.

General Gascoyne, 1806

History, ancient and modern, proves the universal existence of slavery in all countries of Africa ... and this system prevailed ages before the commencement of the European slave trade ... Three-fourths of the Negroes are in a state of slavery [in Africa] ... The European trade in slaves [involves] individuals who are slaves in their own country and if put an end to not one less will exist in Africa.

Mr Hughan, 1807

With regard to the emancipation of the slaves, I have only to say that the opinion of those who have the best local information on the subject is that such a measure would produce the downfall of the Empire.

General Gascoyne, 1807

We have abundance of evidence to prove that during famines which are frequent in Africa, multitudes of the natives fly to slavery as a refuge and without it must inevitably perish ... Here is Africa ... inviting the slave trade, not the slave trade seducing Africa.

Mr Hibbert, 1807

Child labour

[Such intervention] is an imputation on the feelings of parents to suppose that they would suffer their children to work to the prejudice of their health; and it is also an imputation on gentlemen at the head of manufactories to suppose that they would compel children to make excessive exertions.

Mr Curwen, opposing plans for government to legislate on the hours children could work in factories, 1816

At present parents find a difficulty in bringing [children] up well even by the united produce of their labour. The difficulty will be much greater when the children themselves are prevented from contributing anything towards their own support.

Lord Stanley, on the first Factory Act limiting the hours of child labour, 1818

Limiting the hours of labour cannot tend to improve [morals]. On the contrary, it will only give more opportunities for idleness and all the bad consequences arising from it.

Lord Stanley, 1818

I object [to limiting child labour] but so far from considering myself an enemy of the children ... I reckon myself their friend [since] they are improved in health, number and comfort by the free disposal of their labour. If their hours of working are reduced, their wages likewise must be reduced and then they might be exposed to the hardships of want. ... Under the present system the children have labour, food and clothing; under the proposed one they will have idleness, poverty and wretchedness.

Earl of Rosslyn, 1819

The result must be that the [adult workers], unable to bear this greater reduction in the wages of the children [below the minimum age] will be compelled to work their children above that age a greater number of hours than before ... and adults instead of obtaining relief might have to work for fourteen or sixteen hours. This will prove more injurious than the existing system.

Colonel Torrens, 1833

I mistrust that interference on behalf of the poor which the poor are themselves to pay for.

Dr Bowring, 1836

I must say that practical benevolence is more praiseworthy than mistaken humanity. ... See then the blessed effect of the change – the price to be paid for the purchase of 'moral' feeling. Morality is all very well; but will it flourish in beggary and starvation?

Marquess of Londonderry, 1842

Will morals be improved as degrading poverty advances? Will education spread when wages become lower? Will manners become more civilized and will religion penetrate the masses when discontent has taken the place of prosperity and when ease and comfort have given place to despair?

Sir James Graham, Home Secretary, opposing restrictions on child labour, 1844

Education

To carry the system of education to the labouring poor ... will ... raise their minds above their lot in life and by no means strengthen their attachments to those laborious pursuits by which they are to earn a livelihood.

George Rose, vice-president of the Board of Trade, 1807

I do not think ... that the occupiers of lands and houses should be taxed in order that all the children in the country should be taught to read and write, especially when it is doubtful whether writing will be of any real use.

Nicholas Vansittart, secretary of the Treasury, 1807

[Education for the poor] is more pregnant with mischief than advantage ... it will teach [the poor] to despise their lot in life instead of making them good servants in agriculture and other laborious employments to which their rank in society has destined them. Instead of teaching them subordination, it will render them factious and refractory [and] insolent to their superiors.

Mr Giddy, 1807

It is a good people and not a gabbling people that is wanted in the country, and this smattering of education will only raise the labourers of this country above the situations best suited to their own interests ... It will put into their heads that they were not born to labour but to get their living without it.

William Cobbett, 1834

In short, if all are to be scholars, it will be necessary for the whole population to shut up their mouths and determine to eat no more. The interference with labour will be [the] very worst course which can be pursued by the legislature.

Cobbett, 1834

I do not believe ... it will be possible if desirable, or desirable if possible, to establish a system of compulsory education in this country.

Lord Brougham, 1837

I do not think such a system would be palatable in this country ... a system of national compulsory education might do very well for a country in which the government is truly despotic but I do not think that it would do well for such a country like this.

Sir Benjamin Hall, 1847

To give education gratuitously will only degrade the education so given in the estimation of the parents.

Lord Robert Montagu, opposing free education, 1870

It would be a very dangerous thing for us to … take upon ourselves as the state the burden of the education of the children of any portion of the population … We would in effect say to the great body of parents throughout the country, 'We think it our business rather than yours to educate your children,' and I do not think we would be serving the cause of education by allowing such a belief …

William Forster, vice-president of the Council and minister responsible for education, piloting his Education Act of 1870

I consider it a most dangerous thing to convert a nation of labourers into a nation of clerks.

Mr Sandford, 1876

It has been said that children should be kept at school until fourteen years of age; but the amount and importance of the labour which lads between ten and fourteen can perform should not be ignored. Since the present educational system has come into operation, the weeds have very much multiplied in Norfolk which was once regarded as quite the garden of England, weeding being particularly the work of children whose labour is cheap, whose sight is keen, bodies flexible and fingers nimble.

Earl Fortescue, 1880

We ought ... to be very careful ... that the people shall not have put before them by Parliament a fresh lesson that a man may marry as early as he likes and bring as many children into the world as he likes and that the great-grandmother, the state, is going to relieve him of one burden after another and take away from him every motive to be thrifty.

Mr Howorth, opposing state education, 1891

Parliamentary reform

A just sympathy with the people and a reasonable attention to their desires is no doubt the duty and must ever be the inclination of this House. The people, unquestionably, can reason fair when they have time; but, as notoriously their first impulse is feeling, I do not think it would be politic or for the interest of the country to have this House quite subject to popular control.

George Canning, former Foreign Secretary, and Prime Minister to be, 1810

What the present composition of parliament enables us to do is ... to separate the real permanent sense of the people from their hasty passing impressions and to keep up that right of appeal from present passion to future judgement which is necessary in order to preserve us from all the horrors and absurdities of democratic government.

Mr Ward, on the pre-reformed electoral system which gave the vote to 3 per cent of the population, 1812

It is impossible that an assembly, purely democratic, could exist with safety to [the] country. Its measures would vacillate at every variation of popular opinion, however ill-founded ... it would soon become the base pander of the basest passions of the people.

Mr Giddy, 1812

I am decidedly for opposing the beginning of a system which must end in national destruction. [It is] pregnant with the most fatal consequences.

George Canning, 1817

None but persons having means and opportunity and time to cultivate an intimacy with the voters in some district of the country can ever hope to obtain a seat in the House. The lawyer and the banker and the merchant therefore must bid farewell to these walls for ever.

Mr Shelley, 1831

Under such a system, all who have the real and permanent good of their country at heart must tremble for its future state ... [democratic reform will] lead on to a state of anarchy, confusion and ruin and inflict the most serious evils upon all classes of society from the peasant in his cottage to the king on his throne.

Mr Trevor, opposing the Reform Bill, 1832

It is my belief that every general election under such circumstances must be attended with serious riots in all parts of the metropolis.

Sir Richard Vyvyan, 1832

I am convinced that it will be found impossible to make any considerable innovation in the principles of representation which will not expose the country to dangers of the greatest magnitude whilst, on the other hand, it can at best confer upon us a very small and precarious advantage.

Marquis of Bristol, opposing the Reform Bill, 1832

That fatal drollery called a representative government.
Benjamin Disraeli, *Tancred*, 1847

The education fitting a man to decide on the important interests and mighty questions involved in the government of a great nation can never be acquired by those who, because they are earning their daily bread by daily toil, can never possess the leisure for study or for thought.
Earl of Harrowby, 1852

You could not find any point to stop at short of the absolute sovereignty of the people.
Benjamin Disraeli, objecting to electoral reform, 1853

I doubt very much whether a democracy is a government that would suit this country.
Disraeli, 1865

[The result of widening the franchise would be] a Parliament of no statesmanship, no eloquence, no learning, no genius. Instead of these, you will have a horde of selfish and obscure mediocrities, incapable of anything but mischief ... devised and regulated by the raging demagogue of the hour.
Disraeli, opposing reform, 1866. As Chancellor and Leader of the Commons, he piloted through the Reform Bill giving the vote to working-class householders the following year.

Voting is not a right; voting is a public function. No one has any more right to be a voter than he has to be ... a policeman, or a judge, or Prime Minister.

Lord Cecil, House of Lords, 1931

Secret voting

With the feelings of an Englishman, I protest against this secret and unmanly mode of voting ... I do not think that any public benefit can arise from this change ... Is it desirable that men should make a promise with one hand and break it with the other?

Earl of Darlington, opposing secret voting, 1833

[The] first effect will infallibly be an organized system of spies to ascertain whether persons voted according to their promises which will create heart-burnings and jealousies among the lower classes that must put an end to all social peace and comfort.

Viscount Howick, 1835

The ballot ... will be accompanied with much evil – it will spread fraud and deception throughout the country [and] tend to destroy the love of truth and that spirit of manly and open conduct which is the peculiar characteristic of Englishmen.

Mr Poulter, 1835

I object to it because I think it at variance with the national character ... I think a true Englishman hates doing a thing in secret or in the dark. I do not believe that a majority of Englishmen would consent to give their votes in secret even if the law permitted them to do so ... I say that for men who are charged with the high and important duty of choosing the best men to represent the country in Parliament to go sneaking to the ballot-box, and, poking in a piece of paper, looking round to see that no one could read it, is a course which is unconstitutional and unworthy of the character of straightforward and honest Englishmen.

Lord Palmerston, former Foreign Secretary and Prime Minister to be, address to his electors at the general election, 1852

[A] promise [of a vote to a candidate] will either be given or withheld. If it is given, and if the man votes according to his promise, of what use is your ballot? If the promise is given and broken, what becomes of the improvement in the morality of your electoral system? The ballot will then exercise a degrading ... instead of a beneficial influence. You will be lowering the people instead of raising them in the scale as social and civilized men.

Lord Palmerston, 1854

The majority of the electors will evade the law and give their votes in public; and it will be only the few who will go sneaking to the poll for the sake of screening themselves ... but who will thereby become objects of obloquy and degradation in the eyes of their fellow-countrymen.

Lord Palmerston, 1855

One of the worst results of the system [will be] the destruction of all confidence between man and man.

Mr Cave, 1871

Life peerages

I very much doubt whether many persons will be found to seek for the honour of a life peerage, for it seems to me that it would amount I will not say to an insult but to a very humiliating slight to offer a gentleman a peerage and at the same time to tell him that the title and dignity conferred upon him shall not descend to his son.

Earl of Malmesbury, on the first plan to introduce life peers, 1869. They would not be introduced until 1958.

I do not believe that … representatives of the [commercial or industrial] interests would be willing in any large number to accept seats in this House for they would come in upon a different footing from those among whom they sat and accordingly would feel the position more or less a position of degradation.

Earl of Harrowby, 1869

It appears to me that [those accepting life peerages] would stand in such a false position that no men with the usual amount of pride and self-respect would accept these peerages.

Earl of Malmesbury, 1869

What I fear is this, that you will not strengthen the House of Lords as a legislative body but that you will turn it into a sort of legislative Bath or Cheltenham or perhaps … into a sort of legislative hydropathic establishment where these noble persons will take more care of their constitutions than of the constitution of this House.

Earl of Rosebery, leader of the Opposition in House of Lords, 1888

I have no idea of the kind of persons we are going to get as life peers. I am sceptical about whether we are going to get anybody worth while at all.

Lord Silkin, deputy leader of the Opposition in House of Lords, 1957

Members [of the House of Commons] are, of course, delighted at the thought [of life peerages] because they can elevate their more rumbustious female elements to this House. I hate the idea of your Lordships' House becoming a repository for over-exuberant female politicians and unfortunately we are unable to elevate them further, for that prerogative rests with the Almighty.

Earl Ferrers, 1957

Votes for women

[Women's] vocation is a high one. Their vocation is to make life endurable.

Mr Scourfield, 1870

It is not a disability that women should not have a vote but it is rather a privilege that they should not be mixed up in political strife.

Mr Fowler, 1870

Enfranchise women ... you will find yourselves drifting on a sea of impulsive philanthropy and sentimentalism where you are now at anchor on the principles of political economy ... I must say I doubt, if such a change ... takes place, whether we could discuss questions in this House or in the country with our present calmness or whether Parliament would retain the influence which it owes to its reputation for judicial wisdom.

Mr Beresford Hope, 1870

Reason predominates in the man, emotion and sympathy in the woman and if the female vote makes any noticeable difference in the character of our constituencies the risk is that we will have in the House an excess of the emotional and sentimental element over the logical and reasoning faculty.

Mr Beresford Hope, 1871

The character of the legislation of a woman-chosen Parliament will be the increased importance which would be given to questions of a quasi-social or philanthropic character ... our legislation will develop hysterical and spasmodic features.

Mr Beresford Hope, 1871

We regard woman as something to admire, to reverence, to love; and while we will share with her the happiness of life, we will shield her as far as possible from its harsher and sterner duties ... We will not be parties to dragging her down into the arena of our everyday toil and strife.

Edward Knatchbull-Hugessen, under-secretary for the colonies, 1872

It [is] the business of the man to do the hard work and of the woman to make [the] home bright and cheerful for him.

Mr Bouverie, 1872

The real fact is that man in the beginning was ordained to rule over the woman, and this is an eternal decree which we have no right and no power to alter.

Duke of Northumberland, 1873

I ... come to the conclusion ... that all questions affecting the happiness of the nation ... have been settled; and that, upon the principle that it is always necessary to be doing something, we are about to enter on a period of meddling legislation.

Mr O'Donoghue, opposing electoral reform for women, 1877

All the advantages women possess they obtain by reason of their weakness.

Mr Hanbury, House of Commons, 1878

Women can gain nothing but they will be likely to lose a great deal ... Fancy a Member returning home ... and finding there a politician in petticoats ready to continue the debate! ... [It will result in] a system that will eventually destroy the home.

Henry Raikes, 1879

There are certain ladies of very great intellect, no doubt they are women by accident and they want to assume the position of men. Now I object to legislating for what, with all respect to the ladies, I may call freaks of nature.

Henry Labouchere, 1891

Intellectually women have not the gifts which fit them for being elected. They have got a certain amount of what I might call instinct rather than reason [and] they are impulsive, emotional and have got absolutely no sense of proportion.

Labouchere, 1897

I do not know how domestic bliss is to be continued if a man is perpetually leaving his own wife and visiting another man's wife on the plea that he wanted [her vote]. I think that [the House] would agree with me that that would be a very dangerous state of things.

Labouchere, 1904

I think it might fairly be said that women cannot fulfil the duties of citizenship. Of course, it is not their fault that they are more beautiful than muscular.

Labouchere, House of Commons, 1905

Women have at present such an influence over the actions of men that if they had been really united in the desire for the franchise they would have got it long ago. It is only a few women with masculine minds who take an interest in politics and desire to have votes.

Labouchere, 1905

I am quite certain that if women are introduced into the House it would be useless to debate any point at all because the women will have made up their minds before the debate begins.

Sir Frederick Banbury, 1905

Sensible and responsible women do not want to vote. The relative positions to be assumed by men and women in the working out of our civilization were assigned long ago by a higher intelligence than ours.

Grover Cleveland, former US President, 1905

You will never, whatever you think and whatever excited agitators may think, persuade the English nation to take a step which would result in a majority of voters being women.

Mr Harwood, House of Commons, 1910

Does this country really want to see a mixed House of Commons composed of men and women? ... this must be the natural consequence of giving women the vote ... and if they become Members they are bound to become ministers ... Is it really possible that we should contemplate making such a spectacle of ourselves to the civilized world?

Mr Burdett-Coutts, 1911

There are obvious disadvantages about having women in Parliament. I do not know what is going to be done about their hats. ... How is a poor little man to get on with a couple of women wearing enormous hats in front of him?

Mr Hunt, 1913

I know that the ladies are far cleverer than the men in certain relations of life; but government does not require cleverness; it requires wisdom and judgement and we do not so much expect wisdom and judgement from the ladies as enthusiasm in the pursuit of what they consider right.

Lord Clifford of Chudleigh, 1928

Income Tax

This burden should not be left to rest on the shoulders of the public in time of peace because it should be reserved for the important occasions which, I trust, will not soon recur.

Henry Addington, Prime Minister and Chancellor of the Exchequer, abolishing income tax, 1802.

The nation has so unequivocally expressed their indignation at the degrading and oppressive nature of the tax that I am sure no minister will ever dare to reinflict it on the country.

Mr Jones, on the abolition of income tax, 1802. It was revived the following year.

Old Age Pensions

Any universal scheme for giving pensions to everybody is ... beyond the resources of the state. It would cost such an enormous sum and would involve such an entire disintegration of our whole financial system that it is perfectly impossible to contemplate it as practical legislation.

Joseph Chamberlain, Colonial Secretary, 1899

[Pensions] will not induce to the formation of provident habits among our people or the preservation of that disposition to thrift ... I believe the spirit is growing up amongst the people in the direction of providing for themselves against all the ordinary contingencies of life ... I am convinced that [pensions] will tend in the direction of stopping that steady progress.

Mr Bond, 1902

If ... we say to any workman, 'Drink away as much as you like for when you grow old you shall be supported in comfort at the expense of your colleagues who have not drunk,' then clearly we are subsidizing drunkenness. If we do that we are taxing men who spend their money well in order to subsidize the men who spend their money ill.

Mr Cox, 1907

In my opinion, pensions ... are worse than a waste of public money; they are the greatest possible incentive to the absence of self-reliance and thrift.

Viscount St Aldwyn, 1907

Premium Bonds

In my opinion, the result of your issue of Premium Bonds will be not that you will make a man save who has not saved before but that it will induce a man to gamble who has hitherto saved.

Austen Chamberlain, Chancellor of the Exchequer, on proposals for Bonds, 1919

This is ... a combined appeal to the investing instinct and the gambling instinct. I am sure it will never succeed. Insofar as people are investors they are not gamblers; insofar as they are gamblers they are not investors. ... You will never stand the smallest chance in competing against the regular speculative investment ... The sort of man who gives money to the government is the sort who values security. He will not look at an investment of this kind ... Insofar as your appeal is an appeal to gaming it will be a moral disaster; insofar as it is an appeal to investment it will be a financial failure.

Lord Hugh Cecil, 1919

A squalid raffle.

Harold Wilson, shadow Chancellor of the Exchequer, responding to Harold Macmillan's introduction of Premium Bonds in his 1956 Budget

I regard the Premium Bond as a record low for any statesman in this country. It is an appeal to the least desirable instinct in the community, the instinct of getting something for nothing.

Mr Simmons, 1956

[It is] regrettable that when people could not be induced to invest in the future of their country they should be asked to have a flutter on it.

Dr Mabon, 1956

Holidays

If the House enforces idleness by Act of Parliament on the working classes of this country, we will be initiating a ruinous principle which will tend still further to give the advantages which foreign countries are now obtaining over us in all our great national industries for which, up to this time, this country has been pre-eminent.

Mr Wilson, opposing Bank Holidays, 1875

Decimal currency

If you imposed the decimal coinage in this country, you would have a revolution within a week.

Herbert Asquith, Prime Minister, at the Imperial conference, 1911

Motor Cars

We grow corn, oats, hay and straw. Motors do not eat oats, they do not eat hay and they do not lie on the straw and when horses are done away with, it will not be worth while our growing these agricultural articles of consumption having lost our best customer.

Earl of Wemyss, 1903

Depend upon it, if these motorists and motor cars are not kept in order they will have to leave the roads altogether because in the long run the people will never submit to the intolerable nuisance which has been created.

Mr Cripps, 1903

I do not believe the introduction of motor cars will ever affect the riding of horses; the prophecies that have been made are likely to be falsified as have been those made when the railways were introduced.

Mr Scott-Montagu, 1903

If the use of the horn or warning signal by motorists was forbidden ... they would have to go much slower ... and would not be able, by blowing a horn, to order everybody else out of the way. Their speed would be greatly reduced, they would have to pull up oftener and they would be forced to be a little more considerate of other people.

Lord Willoughby de Broke, proposing the banning of horns on cars as the solution to speeding, 1908

I am not one of those people who believe that speed *per se* is really going to make for dangerous driving on our roads today. ... I do not believe the retention of the speed limit will really have any effect in helping to reduce the number of accidents.

Lord Erskine, supporting a government-inspired Bill to abolish the speed limit for cars, 1930. The limits were reintroduced just four years later after a big increase in accidents.

We must make the motorist feel that when he is discourteous and inconsiderate on the road he is not a British gentleman, and that we are not going to regard him as such.

Herbert Morrison, Minister of Transport, piloting the 1930 abolition Bill

To those who suggest that it is an unreasonable hardship to motorists not to drive above thirty miles an hour in a populated area, I would reply that a careful driver has no pleasure in going faster than that.

Mr Anstruther-Gray, on the Bill to reintroduce speed limits, 1934

I firmly believe that a time is coming when many of the problems we are discussing today are going to solve themselves automatically with quickened reaction, with inherited caution, when an ingrained sense of safety is going to take the place of many of these restrictions and regulations which we now have to impose.

Oliver Stanley, Minister of Transport, in charge of the 1934 Bill

My own view is ... that ultimately we shall have to ration cars. We shall have to have a waiting list and people who want motor cars will have to wait for their turn ... Short of some such method ... I see great difficulties ahead.

Mr Lovat-Fraser, on road congestion, 1935. (At the time there were 224,000 cars; by the start of the 1990s there were twenty *million* and still no rationing.)

Driving tests

It has not hitherto been considered necessary or desirable to amend the law in this respect ... Accidents with motor cars are rarely traceable to incompetence to drive while they are not infrequently associated with undue confidence or occasional recklessness on the part of skilled drivers.

John Burns, President of the Local Government Board, and government spokesman on roads, opposing driving tests, 1911

Any advantage which at first sight might appear likely to result from the institution of tests ... would be outweighed by the expense, difficulties and disadvantages inseparable from any such system.

Colonel Ashley, government roads minister, 1925

As far as I am aware, there is no evidence to show that any substantial proportion of accidents ... is due to any want of capacity on the part of drivers such as would be disclosed by a driving test. A universal test of the kind proposed ... would clearly be expensive and might become perfunctory.

Ashley, 1927

My own belief is that the more skilful a man is, the more dangerous he is because he takes greater risks. What really is wanted is road sense and you will not get that by having examinations.

Lord Banbury, 1929

We are satisfied that driving tests have absolutely no value.

Earl Russell, government roads spokesman, House of Lords, 1929

The reason [some drivers] drive safely is because of inexperience. They take no risks; they go slowly and very carefully. The driver who causes the accident ... is the driver who thinks he can do anything and tries to do it once too often. ... I hope your Lordships will not be led away by the fallacy that imposing these tests would do anything to diminish accidents. That really is a fallacy. I think we should get nothing by it.

Russell, 1929

Compulsory insurance

It seems to me that the only result of compulsory insurance would be that nobody would care and accidents would increase.

Lord Banbury, 1925

I can understand a proposal that no motor should be insured against third party risk. That, I think, is an arguable case, because then every person driving would take special care not to inflict damage to life or limb ... but I can also understand the frame of mind of a man who ... says, 'Well, I am insured against all risks; it does not matter,' and he will go ahead for all he is worth and as likely as not will cause an accident.

Viscount Ullswater, 1925

It is quite natural that ... all reckless motorists should be in favour [of insurance] ... Having paid they are free to do what they like.

Lord Banbury, 1926

To carry out a general scheme of insurance would involve great difficulties. I do not believe it will be possible to come to an agreement with the insurance companies.

Colonel Ashley, government roads minister, 1927

Pedestrian crossings

I do not think it would be practicable to introduce such a system in London.

Colonel Ashley, 1928

[Belisha beacon crossings] are a veritable danger ... A pedestrian standing by one of them can of course see the beacon and also thinks that the driver of an oncoming vehicle can see it as well. He cannot but the result is that the pedestrian ventures on to the road ... and an accident is the result. These beacons therefore instead of increasing the safety of pedestrians will definitely do exactly the reverse.

Sir William Brass, 1934

The military

The spectacle of a regiment of motor cars charging, no doubt would be inspiriting but I do not think such a scheme will be likely to prove any permanent advantage to the army.

Lord Stanley, financial secretary to the War Office, House of Commons,
opposing mechanised military transport, 1901

Ordinary common sense tells us that such machines will probably never be used for the carrying of large bodies of troops and ammunition.

Sir Gilbert Parker, House of Commons, 1909 on mechanized military
transport

I doubt whether at any time the reduction of horses will be as great as one might anticipate. I take it that under no circumstances shall we ever want less than 40,000 for the Expeditionary Forces.

Lt-Col John Seely, under secretary, War Office, House of Commons, 1911.
(He became Secretary of State for War the following year.)

I believe that [the War Ministry] are entirely wrong in thinking that they can substitute tanks for cavalry ... That seems to me to be a most extraordinary misreading of the lessons of the war ... It would be the most extraordinary misconception of the truth to imagine that in applying science to war the first thing to get rid of is the horse. On the contrary, every advance in science has made the horse a more and more indispensable weapon of war. Heavy-artillery fire, heavy-machine-gun fire, gas, aeroplane observation – all these make rapid movement more essential.

(Now Major-General) **John Seely**, former Secretary of State for War, House of Commons, 1921

It is obvious that a tank making a very great noise will give many opportunities to the enemy to conceal themselves. It is quite impossible for tanks to be used with advantage in such terrain as marshy ground or for crossing a river when the bridges have been blown up.

Capt. Holt, House of Commons, 1926

Until we are thoroughly satisfied that horses ... can be dispensed with – and I think it is a fairly long time ahead before they can be dispensed with absolutely – the cavalry will remain as it is.

Tom Shaw, Secretary of State for War, House of Commons, 1931

The cavalry will be able to come into their own when mechanical vehicles have all broken down ... and when possibly the petrol dumps are all exploded.

Brigadier-General Makins MP, House of Commons, 1933

I have had occasion during the past year to study military affairs ... and the more I study them, the more I am impressed by the importance of cavalry in modern warfare.

Alfred Duff Cooper, financial secretary to the War Office, presenting the Army Estimates, House of Commons, March 1934. He was promoted to Secretary of State for War the following year, a post he held until 1937.

I am perfectly convinced that the role of the cavalry is still as important today as it has been throughout the ages.

Major Shaw, House of Commons, 1936

It is only too certain that the time may come when we may require the cavalry arm . ... The total abolition of the cavalry would be a frightful blunder.

Brigadier-General Sir Henry Croft, House of Commons, 1936

Military aviation

I do not think that nations in the future are going to conduct their battles by scattering explosives over houses. That is very unlikely to take place ... It is entirely contrary to all practice to scatter explosives in the way suggested and that such a brutal and futile proceeding would be resorted to is one which we need not contemplate.

Alfred Mond, House of Commons, 1909

It will be possible in another war for London to be wrecked by aircraft attack in twelve hours.

Mr Hudson, House of Commons, 1925

I think it is well also for the man in the street to realize that there is no power on earth that can protect him from being bombed. Whatever people may tell him, the bomber will always get through.

Stanley Baldwin, then Lord President of the Council, House of Commons, 1932

The next war is bound to be a short war. I cannot conceive of any country being able to continue a war for a week after its air force, its aerodromes and its petrol tanks have been destroyed ... The war will be decided ... not in five years, or in five weeks but in five days.

Colonel Josiah Wedgwood, House of Commons, 1934

Broadcasting

Make no mistake about it, the repercussions of this new invention [television] are going to be ... very wholesome because they tend to keep the home together ... It does mean that people stay at home.

Lord Brabazon of Tara, 1950

With the coming of television [the average youth] now stays indoors three or four nights a week. Those who are worried about the problem of growing juvenile delinquency should take some comfort from the fact that here is a medium which can attract the young.

John Rodgers, Conservative member for Sevenoaks (making him Winston Churchill's MP), 1953

In my view a spate of mediocre entertainment will encourage vacuity and increased vacuity will result in the demand for even more mediocre entertainment – and so on until the jungle finally closes in ... I feel sure that if this Bill becomes law future historians will deem it to be one of the most irresponsible measures of modern times.

Lord Strabolgi, opposing commercial television, 1954

This is an age of mass perception and through various media of public communication such as elements of the press, a considerable amount of corruption of consciousness has already taken place; and commercial television will just about sink the ship ... A nation fed on this pap for one generation might as well scrap its educational system and spend the money on asylums.

Lord Noel-Buxton, 1954

I will never reconsider it. It would be shocking to have debates in this House forestalled time after time by expressions of opinion by persons who had not the status or responsibility of Members of Parliament.

Sir Winston Churchill, opposing the broadcasting of Parliament, 1955

It would be highly undesirable for [the BBC] to become a simultaneous debating arena with Parliament. There should be explanation, debate, controversy before, and possibly after, Parliament has dealt with an issue but Parliament is the only grand forum of the nation. Once the matter at issue is under actual discussion there, it should not also be being contested on the ether.

Charles Hill, Postmaster-General, and government broadcasting minister, quoting the words in 1949 of the BBC's own director-general, 1955

A national disaster.

Labour Party pamphlet, *Challenge to Britain*, giving the party's official view on commercial television before its introduction in 1955

An enemy of reasonable culture.

Herbert Morrison, Labour elder statesman, on commercial television.

What a total nonsense this business about an image is.

Sir Alec Douglas-Home, on television, resignation speech to Conservative Party conference, 1965

I am a fan of television as far as sport and ceremonial are concerned. I think it less suited to politics than to anything else. You are dealing with the most complicated issues in a very short time and it is bound to be superficial.

Lord Home, 1988

Civil aviation

The task of fostering civilian aviation in the British Isles will be attended with much difficulty. The fogs and mists and other climatic conditions are a terrible hindrance. Moreover, the country is covered by a network of railways and roads which constitute a most formidable competition with the air ... I should not expect to see a very large or a very rapid development of domestic civil aviation within these islands.

Winston Churchill, Secretary of State for Air, 1921

I do not believe that civil aviation has more than very limited potentialities. I believe it may be made a luxurious and costly mode of travel for a very few rich people. I do not believe it will be able to be brought into use for general transport. ... I believe the aeroplane has little or only a very limited future, the whole of its potentialities are warlike.

Mr Rose, 1923

We in this island shall never fly commercially for more than sixty miles over the island. It will never pay us to fly from London to Glasgow commercially and so all our commercial flying has to be from London to the Channel or from London to the North Sea and then over Europe.

Major Hills, 1928

Civil aviation will never be a commercial proposition in this country. It may be that individuals will continue to use aeroplanes for business and pleasure purposes to an increasing degree but as a commercial proposition I think we are already too well served by our railways.

Capt. Cazalet, 1931

We follow with interest any work that is being done in other countries on jet propulsion, but scientific investigation into the possibilities has given no indication that this method can be a serious competitor to the airscrew-engine combination. We do not consider we should be justified in spending any time or money on it ourselves.

Reply from the Air Ministry, to the British Interplanetary Society, 1934

From America ...

While we have land to labour, let us never wish to see our citizens occupied at a work-bench ... For the general operations of manufacture, let our workshops remain in Europe ... The mobs of great cities add ... to the support of good government as sores do to the strength of the human body.

Thomas Jefferson, then American Ambassador to France and future President, opposing America becoming industrialized, 1784

There is every reason to believe that our system will soon attain the highest degree of perfection of which human institutions are capable.

James Monroe, US President, 1820

Suez canal

It is an undertaking which I believe in point of commercial character may be deemed to rank among the many bubble schemes that from time to time have been palmed upon gullible capitalists.

Lord Palmerston, Prime Minister, on plans to build the Suez canal, 1857

The project for executing a canal across the Isthmus of Suez is a most futile idea – totally impossible to be carried out. It will be attended with a lavish expenditure of money for which there will be no return; and even if successfully carried out in the first instance, the operation of nature will in short time defeat the ingenuity of man.

Benjamin Disraeli, Chancellor of the Exchequer, on the building of the Suez canal, 1858. It opened in 1869 and six years later Disraeli spent £4 million to buy the Egyptian government's shares in it.

It is very much regretted ... that when [England] needs cotton, 30,000 or 40,000 people who might be usefully employed in the cultivation of cotton in Egypt are occupied in digging a canal through a sandy desert ... I should hope that so useless an occupation will soon be put an end to.

Lord Palmerston, Prime Minister, 1864

Science

I am tired of this sort of thing called science. We have spent millions in that sort of thing for the last few years, and it is time it should be stopped.

Simon Cameron, US senator for Pennsylvania, opposing funds for the Smithsonian Institution, 1861

Everything that can be invented has been invented.

Charles Duell, Director of US Patent Office addressing President William McKinley to abolish the office, 1899

10 *Ouch!*

Sitting Ducks

They asked for it ...

When Napoleon retreated from Moscow after his failed invasion of Russia
in 1812, he fled almost alone leaving his army to fend for itself. On
reaching the Neman river

Napoleon (to the ferryman): Have any deserters come through this way?
Ferryman: No, you are the first.

That depends, my Lord, whether I embrace your mistress or your principles.

Attributed to **John Wilkes** (1727–97), responding to Lord Sandwich who
had told Wilkes that he would die either of the pox or on the gallows

The atrocious crime of being a young man, which the honourable
gentleman has with such spirit and decency charged upon me, I shall
attempt neither to palliate nor to deny, but content myself with wishing
that I shall be one of those whose follies shall cease with their youth,
and not of that number who are ignorant in spite of experience.

William Pitt (the Elder), answering the criticism of Robert Walpole, 1741

Yes, I am a Jew, and when the ancestors of the right honourable gentleman were brutal savages in an unknown land, mine were priests in the temple of Solomon.

Benjamin Disraeli, replying to Daniel O'Connell, Irish Catholic leader, who had ridiculed his Jewish ancestry, House of Commons, 1835

Disraeli was once upbraided by the Speaker and asked to withdraw his assertion that 'Half the Cabinet are asses':

Mr Speaker, I withdraw. Half the Cabinet are not asses.

Student leader: We want to talk to you but we think it's impossible for you to understand us. You weren't raised in a time of instant communications or satellites and computers ... we now live in an age of space travel ... jet travel and high speed electronics. You didn't have those things when you were young.
Ronald Reagan: No, we didn't have those things when we were your age – we invented them.

Ronald Reagan, when Governor of California, responding to a group of student demonstrators who had occupied his office

They've got a point. I don't have any experience in running up a $4,000 billion debt.

Ross Perot, responding to George Bush who had accused him of having no experience in government, US presidential campaign, 1992

And when we open our dykes, the waters are ten feet deep.

Queen Wilhelmina of the Netherlands responding to the threatening boast of Kaiser Wilhelm II of Germany shortly before the First World War that 'all my guardsmen are seven feet tall'. (attrib.)

Fourteen? The good Lord only has ten.

Georges Clemenceau, French Prime Minister, responding to US President Woodrow Wilson's announcement to Congress of his Fourteen Points peace plan of January 1918 to end the First World War.

Yes, a relief – like crapping in your pants.

Alexis Leger, French aide at the 1938 Munich conference which sacrificed Czechoslovakia to Hitler, in response to his colleague Paul Stehlin's declaration that 'this agreement is a relief'

At the state banquet during a visit to Brazil, Prince Philip was introduced to a Brazilian general whose uniform was resplendent with medals and who, when Philip enquired, said they had been won in the war:

Philip: I didn't know Brazil was in the war that long.
The general: At least, sir, I didn't get them for marrying my wife.

Viscount Kilmuir: A cook would have been given more notice of his dismissal.
Harold Macmillan: Ah, but good cooks are hard to find.

Prime Minister's riposte to his aggrieved former Lord Chancellor, one of the seven victims of Macmillan's 'night of the long knives' Cabinet reshuffle, July 1962. Kilmuir had been continuously in office for eleven years.

I shall not dance with you for three reasons. First, because you are drunk. Second, because this is not a waltz but the Peruvian national anthem. And third, because I am not a beautiful lady in red; I am the cardinal bishop of Lima.

Legendary attributed response at a diplomatic reception to the drunken behaviour of George Brown, Labour Foreign Secretary 1966–8

Well, I hope your f**king feathers all fall out.

George Brown, to Len Williams, Labour party general secretary who had just been appointed Governor-General of Mauritius by Harold Wilson, 1968. Brown, who disliked Williams, had asked whether his new position required him 'to wear one of those plumed hats.' Williams had replied that it did.

If it's a boy, it will be named after our late King George. If it's a girl, it will be Elizabeth, after our Queen. If, however, it is merely wind, as I suspect, it will be named John Foster Dulles.

Winston Churchill, responding to Dulles, American Secretary of State 1953–9, who had patted his growing stomach and asked, 'When's it due, Winston?' (attrib.)

It's a pity others had to leave theirs on the ground at Goose Green to prove it.

Neil Kinnock, replying during a TV election debate, to a member of the audience who had shouted that Margaret Thatcher 'had guts', 1983. Mr Kinnock points out that there were demands that he withdraw his statement. He didn't, he says, 'not least because several people in, or associated with, the Forces took the trouble to let me know that they thought I should stand by what I said'.

Very well. Good day.

Clement Attlee's response to a young MP, to whom he had offered a post in his government, who had expressed humbleness about his abilities to do the job

He was the father of a President of the United States.

Harry Truman, responding to stories that his father had been a failure

Dewey: I'm glad to see so many children in the crowd. You should be grateful because I got you a day off school.
Child: Today is Saturday!

Thomas Dewey, US Republican candidate, presidential campaign, 1948

★

John F Kennedy talking to a businessman, trying to counter a prevailing mood of pessimism in the business world in 1961:

Things look great. Why, if I wasn't President, I'd be buying stock myself.
Businessman: If you weren't President, so would I.

★

In your heart, you know he's right.

Election slogan of Republican candidate Barry Goldwater, presidential campaign 1964

In your guts, you know he's nuts.

Democratic Party opponent's response, 1964

★

Dole in 96.

Republican bumper sticker, American presidential campaign, 1996

Dole IS 96.

Democrat bumper sticker, 1996

★

Prime Minister Stanley Baldwin was sitting in a railway compartment with one other traveller, who stared at him intently before he leaned over and tapped his knee.

Man: You're Baldwin, aren't you? You were at Harrow in '84
Baldwin: Yes, you're right.
Man (after a long pause): Tell me, what are you doing now?

Quoted by Roy Jenkins, *Baldwin*, 1987

Roy Jenkins's travels in search of a seat after forming the SDP took the new party leader to Glasgow Hillhead in March 1982. Canvassing in the by-election, he approached a man of Indian extraction, asking:

Jenkins: How long have you been here?
Man: A lot longer than you.

When Uncle Jack was your age, he was President of the United States.

Schoolboy, to 1972 Democratic vice-presidential candidate Sargent Shriver, a Kennedy in-law, who tried to inspire the class to work harder by telling them that Abraham Lincoln at their age had walked twelve miles back and forth to school every day.

After each of my foreign trips, I have made recommendations which were adopted.

Richard Nixon, Republican presidential candidate, who had been Eisenhower's Vice-President for eight years, attempting to stress his experience over opponent John F Kennedy, campaign, 1960

If you give me a week, I might think of one.

President Eisenhower, to reporters who asked what these had been, 1960

George Bush doesn't have the manhood to apologize.

Walter Mondale, election debate between Vice-Presidents, 1984

Well, on the manhood thing, I'll put mine up against his any time.

George Bush's response, 1984

Representative Anne Mueller: Mr Speaker, will you please turn me on.
House Speaker, Tom Murphy: Thirty years ago, I would have tried.

Exchange in the Georgia state assembly, after Mueller had complained that
her microphone was switched off

Like many car accidents, they are a matter of perception.

Bob Packwood, US senator for Oregon, accounting for twenty-nine
accusations of sexual harassment against him, TV interview, March 1994

Forgive me, Senator, but when you have twenty-nine car crashes,
there's something wrong with the way you're driving.

Barbara Walters, the interviewer, March 1994

American workers should draw a mushroom cloud and put underneath
it: 'Made in America by lazy and illiterate Americans and tested in
Japan.'

Ernest Hollings, US senator for South Carolina, responding to remarks by
Yoshio Sakurauchi, speaker of the Japanese Parliament, who attacked the
American workforce as lazy and illiterate, 1992

Princess Diana, during a walkabout in South Australia in 1983, tousled the hair of a little boy in the crowd.

Princess: Why aren't you at school today?
The boy: I was sent home because I've got head lice.

We've got a corporal at the top, not a cavalry officer.

Francis Pym, Foreign Secretary, on Margaret Thatcher, 1982. The remark, made privately, reached her ears, enraging her. It may have helped seal his fate.

Landslides, on the whole, don't produce successful governments.

Pym, general election campaign, 1983. This did seal his fate

There is an ex-chief Whips' club. They are very unusual people

Margaret Thatcher's response, the following day. Pym was returned to the back benches immediately after the election

During a filibuster on the Antarctic Minerals Bill, July 1989:

Mr Hardy (Wentworth, Lab): I asked Lech Walesa ... Lech Walesa does not speak English, but he stuck his thumb up and gave me a broad grin ...
The Deputy Speaker: Order. I think that the hon Gentleman is on the wrong Pole.

That is a higher proportion than the percentage of the general public with whom I am familiar.

Peter Lilley, Trade and Industry Secretary, responding to barracking that, according to a survey, only 2 per cent of the British public actually knew who he was, 1990

Graham Allen (Nottingham North, Lab): To ask the Lord President of the Council, how many parliamentary questions have been answered in the past twelve months with the statement that the required figures are not available.
Tony Newton: This information is not in a readily available form and could only be provided at disproportionate cost.

Hansard, November 1993

Dennis Skinner (Lab, Bolsover): To ask the Minister for the Civil Service, how many civil servants in employment at the latest date are (a) men or (b) women.
Tim Renton: All of them.

Hansard, February 1992

George Ealloway: Why do people take such an instant dislike to me?
A colleague: Because it saves time.

Reported exchange, 1992

The hon. Lady was once an egg and people on both sides of this House greatly regret its fertilization.

Sir Nicholas Fairbairn, to Edwina Currie, junior health minister, during the salmonella in eggs scare sparked by her comments, 1988

Rejoice! Rejoice!

Margaret Thatcher, after the recapture of South Georgia during the Falklands War, 1982

Rejoice! Rejoice!

Sir Edward Heath, after Margaret Thatcher's defeat in the Conservative
leadership contest, 1990

They're from my husband's funeral.

Response to an MP, whose identity was not disclosed, canvassing in the
Kincardine and Deeside by-election, who had 'offered fulsome
congratulations on the stunning floral display in the constituent's hallway',
The Times report, 1991

11 *Aha!*

Transparent Euphemisms

Public life can infect its denizens with a pathological inability to spit it out. Who did these people think they were kidding? ...

I do not like this word 'bomb'. It is not a bomb. It is a device which is exploding.

Jacques Le Blanc, French ambassador to New Zealand, responding to criticism of France's nuclear tests in the Pacific, October 1995

The war situation has developed, not necessarily to Japan's advantage.

Emperor Hirohito announcing the Japanese surrender after the dropping of the two atomic bombs, national broadcast, 1945

[Nuclear war is] something that may not be desirable.

Ed Meese, counsellor in the Reagan White House, 1982

This is not war. The marines are not in combat.

White House response to Congressional attempts to vote to withdraw US troops from Beirut after the first fatalities in the peacekeeping force in August 1983. Under the War Powers Act, Congress could invoke its rights only in war conditions

The crucial point is that they are in a stationary position.

Further White House elaboration when Congressional leaders asserted that war conditions did exist since American troops were returning fire, 1983

Nothing has changed. We are not leaving Lebanon. The marines are being deployed two or three miles to the west.

Caspar Weinberger, US Defence Secretary, denying in 1984 that the movement of US troops amounted to a retreat. The deployment 'two or three miles to the west' just happened to be from land bases on Lebanese soil to ships offshore.

We are not at war with Egypt. We are in armed conflict.

Sir Anthony Eden, Prime Minister, after the Anglo–French landings in Suez, 1956

We were not micro-managing Grenada intelligence-wise until about that time-frame.

US Admiral **Wesley McDonald**, explaining why America was taken by surprise by the coup on Grenada in 1983, which prompted the US airborne invasion (which was officially termed not an invasion but '*a pre-dawn vertical insertion*').

'Burnham Category II/III courses may or may not be advanced and poolable. A Burnham Category II/III course which is not poolable is not poolable only because it is not advanced, i.e. it does not require course approval as an advanced course. It is therefore wrong to ascribe it as a "non-poolable advanced (non-designated) course". Non-poolable courses are non-advanced by definition. I think that the problem you have described probably results from confusion here.'

'Explanatory' letter from the Department of Education and Science, quoted by **Lord Elwyn Jones**, House of Lords, 1987

The slowing in the universities' rate of expansion experienced in the 1970s was replaced in the early 1980s by an expenditure-led policy of contraction.

Government report on university funding, *Review of the University Grants Commission*, chaired by Lord Croham, deploying an elegant euphemism for spending cuts, February 1987

We have not closed down our parties – just suspended their activities.

General Kenan Evren, Turkish military ruler, 1981

I did not desire to fire Mr Fitzgerald. I prefer to use the correct term: which is to abolish his job.

Robert Seamons, US Secretary for the Air Force, dismissing Ernest Fitzgerald, an efficiency expert who had identified massive overspending, 1969

A wage-based premium.

President Clinton, pledged not to raise taxes, announcing the means (taxation) by which his health care plan would be financed, 1993

User fee.

President Reagan's administration, also pledged not to raise taxes, describing the four cents a gallon increase in the federal petrol tax, 1983

A very large, potentially disruptive re-entry system.

Pentagon description of the Titan II nuclear missile, 600 times more powerful than the Hiroshima bomb, 1980s

[The test] was terminated five minutes earlier than planned [after the missile] impacted the ground prematurely.

US Air Force explanation of a cruise missile crash, 1986

Rapid oxidation; energetic disassembly; abnormal evolution.

Terminology introduced by the US nuclear power industry after the 1979 Three Mile Island accident for official reporting of incidents. The terms were to be used instead of 'fire', 'explosion' and 'accident'.

[The suspect was] eliminate[d] with extreme prejudice.

CIA description of its execution of a suspected double agent in Vietnam, 1971

This is the operative statement. The others are inoperative.

Ronald Ziegler, Nixon press secretary, after the President had admitted the involvement of senior White House aides in the Watergate cover up, reminded by reporters of previous statements denying involvement, April 1973

The ministry cancels this portion of the minister's remarks as non-existent.

South Korean Defence Ministry statement sanitizing Lee Jong-Koo's remarks when he publicly advocated military raids on North Korean nuclear facilities, April 1991

An incomplete success.

President Jimmy Carter describing the failed attempt to rescue the US embassy hostages held in Iran, 1980

It is a tricky problem to find the particular calibration in timing that would be appropriate to stem the acceleration in risk premiums created by falling incomes without prematurely aborting the decline in the inflation-generated risk premiums.

Alan Greenspan, chairman of the President's Council of Economic Advisers, testifying to a Senate committee why the Nixon administration's anti-inflation policies weren't working, 1974

I guess I should warn you, if I turn out to be particularly clear, you've probably misunderstood what I've said.

Greenspan, then chairman of the Federal Reserve Board, speech to the Economic Club, 1988

We have no political prisoners. We have political internal exiles.

Chilean President **Augusto Pinochet**, 1975

It became necessary to destroy the village in order to save it.

US Army report on the razing of Ben Tre, South Vietnam, 1968

It was not a bombing of Cambodia. It was a bombing of North Vietnamese in Cambodia.

Henry Kissinger, 1973

You always write it's bombing, bombing, bombing. It's not bombing, it's air support.

Colonel David Opfer, US Air Force attaché at the American embassy in Cambodia, to journalists, 1974

We are conducting limited duration protective reaction air strikes.

US Army spokesman, Vietnam, describing a bombing campaign

Let's push this to a lower decibel level of public fixation.

Alexander Haig, US Secretary of State, 1981–2, ordering a campaign to reduce public awareness of a particular government policy

I do not deny that torture continues to be used in this country, but there are strict orders to the army not to use torture.

General Ernesto Geisel, military President of Brazil, 1974–9

You won the election; but I won the count.

Anastasio Somoza, dictator of Nicaragua, 1967–79, to his defeated opponent in the fixed presidential election which ushered in his regime. His family dynasty had ruled the country since 1937.

I didn't accept it. I received it.

Richard Allen, national security adviser to President Reagan, explaining how he came to gain $1,000 and two watches from journalists in return for an exclusive interview with Mrs Reagan

We have no political prisoners – only Communists and others involved in conspiracies against the country.

Park Chung Hee, President of South Korea, 1974

Outside of the killings, we have one of the lowest crime rates.

Marion Barry, Mayor of Washington DC, the city with the highest murder rate in America, 1989

I haven't committed a crime. What I did was fail to comply with the law.

David Dinkins, Mayor of New York, fending off accusations of tax evasion.

It should be made quite clear that pharmacists are not striking for more money but for an improved rate of pay for their profession.

Michael Beaman, Guild of Hospital Pharmacists Council, 1982

It was not a defeat. I was merely placed third in the polls.

Bill Pitt, first successful Liberal/SDP Alliance candidate, after winning the Croydon NW by-election in 1981, on his previous attempt to win the seat at the 1979 general election. (How he described his non-defeat in 1983, when he finished second to the Conservative, is not recorded.)

Epilogue

Humour is not much fun. If you give it a moment's thought, at the root of any kind of humour – literary, theatrical, televisual – you will likely find suffering. When we find situations amusing, it is usually because we are watching misfortune being inflicted on a fellow human being. Countless theatrical farces and TV sitcoms testify to this apparent paradox. We laugh because someone else is hurting. The Germans (who else?) even have their own word for it, *schadenfreude,* literally joy from harm, that glorious self-indulgent pleasure in another's plight.

It is one thing to take delight at another's embarrassment when it is simply the dictate of Fate which has decreed that calamity should befall them and not us. We have a sense of relief – 'there but for the grace of God ... ' But even richer is the feast of *schadenfreude* when the victim has brought about his or her own downfall. This collection has been intended for those (actually, most of us, if we are honest with ourselves) who enjoy seeing the famous, the not-so-famous, and those who just feel they *ought* to be famous, have their come-uppance from their own lips.

Politics is perhaps the ideal, most fertile ground for a harvest of this kind. Politics *is* about articulating viewpoints clearly, about assessing trends and seeing the way ahead clearly, and about saying the right thing in the right place at the right time. The major problem is that a lot of politicians are not very good at it. This is doubly ironic, as they imagine themselves (and we elect them to be) more closely in touch with the pulse and direction of national life than us mere mortals.

In 1775, Samuel Johnson wrote that politics was nothing more than a means of rising in the world. This compilation, from the lips of the great, the good and the awesomely incompetent, may have suggested that it can be just as easily the most potent means of falling too. Some of the most august names appear here – even Winston Churchill whose perspicacity about the threat to peace in the 1930s has become the defining contrast to the short-sightedness of his appeasing contemporaries. It is comforting to know he, too, went awry at times.

It was Churchill, no less, who also famously offered his definition of the job requirement for a politician. 'It is,' he said, 'the ability to predict what is going to happen tomorrow, next week, next month, and next year,' – then adding after a telling pause – 'and to have the ability afterwards to explain why it didn't happen.'

We have not been too concerned here with the wriggling afterwards. The words first uttered speak with sufficient volume, and give an insight into incompetence that no post-humiliation rationalizing can remove.

Is there a cure? We seriously hope not, for it would remove the little joy derivable from what is so often a depressingly sterile business. Many here might well have been advised to take a lesson from the no-nonsense approach of US President Lyndon Johnson. During the Vietnam era, he often visited military bases around the country to give rousing send-offs to GIs embarking for the war. At one, in 1966, he told the men that he was proud that his great-great-grandfather had perished at the Alamo – which was totally untrue. When his press officer suggested he retract, he said, 'I never said that.' When told that everyone had just heard him say it, he offered the definitive method of extracting foot from mouth: 'I don't give a damn what you heard. I did not say it. I can state categorically that my great-great-grandfather did not die at the Alamo.' One helluva cheek.

We hope you have enjoyed the others quoted here. If any feeling of guilt about pleasuring in their folly crept up upon you as you read, remember this. They willingly put themselves up for your judgement. Judge them, and have no mercy.

Phil Mason